Management of
Expanding Enterprises

Management of
Expanding Enterprises

REPORT OF ROUND TABLE DISCUSSIONS
BY LEADING BUSINESS AND PROFESSIONAL MEN

BY *William H. Newman*

SAMUEL BRONFMAN PROFESSOR
OF DEMOCRATIC BUSINESS ENTERPRISE
GRADUATE SCHOOL OF BUSINESS, COLUMBIA UNIVERSITY

AND *James P. Logan*

ASSISTANT PROFESSOR OF BUSINESS ADMINISTRATION
AMOS TUCK SCHOOL OF BUSINESS ADMINISTRATION
DARTMOUTH COLLEGE

NEW YORK AND LONDON   COLUMBIA UNIVERSITY PRESS

*This project was carried out under a grant from
the McKinsey Foundation for Management Research*

Round Table on Management of Expanding Enterprises

Marvin Bower, Managing Partner, McKinsey & Company

John T. Connor, Administrative Vice-President, Merck & Company

Carle C. Conway, Chairman, Executive Committee, Continental Can Company

Peter F. Drucker, Writer, Consultant, Professor of Management, New York University

John M. Fox, President, Minute Maid Corporation

Edwin T. Gibson, Executive Director, The American Assembly, Columbia University (formerly Executive Vice-President, General Foods Corporation)

Reginald E. Gillmor, Vice-President, Sperry Corporation

William B. Given, Chairman of the Board, American Brake Shoe Co.

Joseph A. Grazier, President, American Radiator & Standard Sanitary Corp.

Philip B. Hofmann, Vice-Chairman of the Board, Johnson & Johnson

A. W. Hughes, President, J. C. Penney Company

Elmer L. Lindseth, President, The Cleveland Electric
Illuminating Company
Gerald J. Lynch, Director, Office of Defense Products and
Governmental Research, Ford Motor Company
Wayne Marks, Vice-President, General Foods Corpora-
tion
Ewing W. Reilley, Partner, McKinsey & Company
Oren Root, Partner, Hatch, Root, Barrett, Cohen & Knapp
John A. Sargent, President, Diamond Alkali Company
Wallace Sayre, Government Consultant, Professor of Pub-
lic Administration, Columbia University
Harold F. Smiddy, Vice-President, General Electric Com-
pany

William H. Newman, Chairman
James P. Logan, Secretary

Preface

EVERY year millions of dollars are invested in scientific research and training of technical specialists. The tremendous technical advances of the last few years bear witness that this use of our resources was indeed wise. There is, however, a serious lack of balance in our research activities. We are giving too little attention to our fund of knowledge about the *management* of these new processes and technical specialists.

The exploration reported in this book delves into a phase of management where the potential rewards of research are high. Management of large-scale enterprises is the center of attention; here we find that success and growth have created new challenges for top administrators. Relatively little is known in this field, and a distinctive method was used in this study to uncover the central issues. The aim of the study is to identify the major problems, find where men of experience agree or disagree on an effective course of action, and block out areas where further research is likely to be especially fruitful.

This undertaking has been very much a cooperative endeavor. A grant by the McKinsey Foundation for Management Research to the Graduate School of Business at

Columbia University made the study possible, and the generous contribution of time and energy by members of the Round Table provided insights obtainable from no other source. The authors are grateful for the opportunity to try to capture some of the wisdom of experience brought to light by this joint venture.

WILLIAM H. NEWMAN

JAMES P. LOGAN

January, 1955

Contents

Management of
Expanding Enterprises

Introduction

THE FUTURE of the free enterprise system depends to a large degree upon the skill with which individual enterprises are managed. To be sure, we also need an economic environment which encourages many separate firms to seek new ways of fulfilling consumer wants. Such an economic environment provides the setting, but the initiative—the spark necessary to change potentialities into realities—comes from the management of individual firms.

Management of an enterprise is predominantly a matter of people and their relationships with each other. The managers themselves are people. Their job is to guide the cooperative efforts of other people toward the common objective. Managing is primarily a social activity; and, like other social processes, the study of management is of fairly recent origin.

In most business firms, management techniques tend to be perpetuated by one business generation after another. As new problems arise or as outside firms find a new management process which is well suited to their particular need, adjustments may be made. All too often, however, the sound thinking that may go into such adjustments is not fully appreciated by the next generation of executives.

Even less frequently is the successful experience analyzed into basic concepts or principles that may be helpful in dealing with new situations.

THE ROUND TABLE APPROACH

The following pages report an endeavor to improve our understanding of the management of modern enterprises. A group of outstanding business and professional men met for a series of discussions on the "management of expanding organizations." The members, whose names appear in the front of this book, included top executives with richly varying experience in directing business undertakings as well as a number of professional men who had close relationships with many other firms. While most of this experience has been in the business field, there was also a substantial background in governmental and military operations. The aim of the discussions was to capture some of this wisdom regarding management which this group of eminent men has developed.

These round tables were a serious effort to push back the frontiers of knowledge about managing expanding enterprises. The frank exchange of views brought out many ideas and called forth observations that would have been hard to get in any other way.

AREA EXPLORED

Attention was focused on large-scale enterprises. These are companies which have outgrown the capacity of a single executive, or a small group of top executives, to run as a closely integrated operation. Members of the Round Table stated repeatedly that their most difficult problems arose when the management techniques which had been so useful in guiding companies of one, two, or three thousand employees became inadequate for the task of administering their growing and ramified operations.

Generally speaking, there appear to be three critical stages of growth of a company. The first and clearest change occurs in a small store or shop when a skilled craftsman turns most of the actual operations over to his helpers. He tries to get things done through the efforts of other people rather than doing them himself. He becomes a manager, at least to the extent that he learns the art of delegation. It is true, of course, that some firms by-pass this first stage: the original organizers start out as managers of a small group of employees.

In small companies, the chief executive knows all of the operations intimately; he may perform some of these himself or at least he is able to give specific direction to workers and to supervisors. Many a self-made businessman has shown a remarkable capacity to continue this type of management even though his usefulness has long since outgrown the confines of a single shop or a small store. Nevertheless, as expansion continues, and especially when some unusually gifted president withdraws from active leadership, a new type of management is required. The transformation is indeed critical for most companies. Organization becomes more specialized and more formalized; greater reliance is placed on records and reports; budgets may be introduced as a means for planning and coordination; systematic attention may be given to the development of executives; and a whole array of other modern management techniques are used by the top executives of the company. This second type of transition is by no means easy but at least we think we know something about it.

The third critical stage of company growth, from a management point of view, arises when the magnitude, diversity, and complexity of activities makes management by these familiar tools unwieldy. There are too many specialists to be consulted and coordinated. The volume of reports is so great that they receive scant attention. A top executive no longer is sufficiently familiar with operations to really use the budget as a planning device. Junior executives become names and statistics rather than personalities. Again, a fundamental shift in management philosophy is called for.

Expansion to this size inevitably raises questions not only of decentralization and use of staff but also of methods of planning, kinds of executives needed, types of control, and similar issues.

Surprisingly little is known about the principles of managing enterprises when they pass into this third stage of growth. To be sure, the management techniques followed by General Motors and a few of the other large firms have been described, studies of separate activities are available, and three or four senior executives from large companies have found time to write down their thinking about management, but much more analysis is needed.

SIGNIFICANCE OF SUBJECT

The management of these large enterprises is of critical importance to our scale of living and to the strength of the nation. While there are only about 250 firms in the United States which employ more than ten thousand employees, these firms provide almost one fifth of the total paid employment in the country. There are additional firms with somewhat smaller payrolls which present similar administrative problems because of their widespread or diverse activities.

Any such large segment of the economy affects directly or indirectly every village from the Atlantic to the Pacific. The health of these firms has an influence upon literally hundreds of thousands of dealers, parts suppliers, and service operations. Moreover, because of their size, these firms are expected to show true business leadership.

The effective management of these large concerns is of vital interest to all of us.

A healthy economy needs strength in all of its major parts. The millions of small firms and the thousands of middle-sized ones are vital to our flexible dynamic society. In singling out large-scale enterprises for special study, we are simply saying that this type of business is also of great importance and that it happens to be an area where our knowledge is limited.

AIM OF THE ROUND TABLE

The specific purpose of these round table discussions was to block out major issues, note where substantial agreement exists, and identify areas where further research promises to be particularly fruitful. The round table technique is peculiarly well suited to this broad type of exploration. It is provocative, suggestive, and stimulating. Frank, informal discussion among able men often brings out new facets of problems.

It was not intended that these round tables try to arrive

at a definitive answer on any particular issue. This would have limited our scope and called for much more factual investigation. Instead, we tried to probe and explore and to take a fresh look at the nature of the management task in expanding enterprises.

Among the issues discussed were the following:

How are the processes of planning affected by size? For example, does the real meaning of "policy" change as companies expand?

What happens to standards used to measure executive performance, and what new problems of measurement arise?

Are there any patterns of departmental organization best adapted to different stages of growth or size?

What are the opportunities and limitations of decentralized location of activities?

How does size affect "identification" (bureaucracy) and morale of employees at various organization levels?

What are the opportunities for, and the need for, staff work in expanding organizations?

What arrangements, formal and informal, can be made to overcome communication difficulties?

How does size affect the opportunities, and obstacles, for personal initiative?

Can flexibility be achieved in large-scale operations? This relates to sensitiveness, speed, and cost.

To what extent can control be secured through indoctrination, selective executive promotion, and other indirect ways of shaping the thoughts of subordinates?

When should self-contained operating units be introduced? How far should independence go?

How does size affect the kinds of executives needed at various organization levels? How does it affect the task of discovery and development of such executives?

To guide our deliberations, an agenda with only three or four leading questions was circulated in advance of each of the eight dinner meetings. The resulting discussion was brisk and to the point. Average attendance was fourteen; that is, most, but not all, members of the group were able to come to each session.

This report of the round table discussions is definitely a composite of the views expressed. Since the conversation was frank and off-the-record, ideas in the following report are not identified with individuals. Instead, a general digest is given. This digesting of the discussions inevitably squeezes out some of their liveliness, but it also makes the report shorter and easier for the reader to get at the kernel of the thoughts presented.

On some points there were sharp differences, as will be indicated in the following chapters. But there was a common conviction on this: the future success of our free enterprise system depends to a significant degree upon the skill top executives develop for dealing with increasing size of operations.

1

Effect of Company Size on Management Tasks

WHEN is a company "big"? More specifically, does bigness change the job of key executives? If so, at what stages in company growth do the tasks of management shift?

These questions about company size have no single, simple answer. As members of the Round Table told of their experiences in dealing with size, the need for understanding the reasons and nature of growth of the specific enterprise quickly became apparent. Adding stores to a retail chain, for instance, creates administrative problems quite different from those faced by a steel producer who has just decided to develop foreign sources of ore. Consequently, discussion at the first meeting turned to the reasons for large size.

THE "WHY" OF LARGE ENTERPRISES

A background of the why and how of big business is helpful (a) to the executive who must deal with a concrete problem created by size and (b) to those seeking principles (useful generalizations) which apply in a variety of situations.

Common reasons for large size, brought out in our consideration of management of growing enterprises, included:

a) Demands of customers. Sometimes the customer decides the size—especially when large customers demand, and many other customers want, to be served everywhere. Manufacturers of tin cans, for example, have found it desirable to operate plants in all parts of the country so that they could fill all the needs of large food packers. Similarly, airlines prefer to deal with oil companies which can provide an assured supply of fuel at all major airports.

b) To master a particular technology. The manufacture of an end product may force a company to engage in large-scale integration or to control whole chains of technology, e.g., steel or automobile production. One member observed that the technological cost of having separate, specialized divisions was the real drive to a unified Defense Department in the Federal government.

c) To take full advantage of research. A member noted that in the chemical business the diversification problem is tied up with research. The research department may turn up a product which is outside the company's particular line. Then there arises the basic management problem of whether the new product is going to be pursued.

d) To market goods effectively. Another reason mentioned was to serve the whole U.S. and Canadian market, or to take full advantage of an advertised brand name. For example, the need for a "full line" for distributors has fostered the handling of television sets, radios, refrigerators, washing machines, and other appliances by firms which originally produced only a single product. Toothpaste companies add shaving cream or shampoos in order to capitalize on their brand reputation.

e) Moreover, it was suggested that able management led inevitably to size. A company cannot stand still, and a successful effort to avoid slipping backward means that the good companies tend to get big.

Any one of these reasons for growth may well be a vital factor in the kind of management best suited to the expanded operations. As noted in the next chapter, for instance, semiautonomous units may be desirable for exploitation of a new product coming out of the research laboratory whereas expansion to use a new technological process often calls for closer integration of activities. Useful guides for the management of large enterprises must, then, be sufficiently flexible to permit a firm to retain the economic advantage which lies back of its expansion.

There is also the corollary issue of whether a company can get too big. This question has two parts: should the size of the total enterprise be limited or just the size of operating divisions?

One member made the point that it was possible to keep the small type of operating management by multiplying rather than by expanding the initial unit. Another replied: "We know for sure that people are afraid of size. There is a real issue as to how big in total we should become." On this point, the justification for a company with semiautonomous operating divisions was challenged. "What do you gain by operating as you do? Each decentralized operating division is a full-scale business in itself. Why don't you incorporate each of the 10 businesses, turn them loose, float their stock on the general market, and set the top office up as a consulting business? Let them buy your consulting services if they desire."

In general, the group felt that even the billion dollar corporations were economically desirable. Benefits noted included ease of financing, ability to take large risks, stable profits and dividends while one division was going through a development or reorganization stage, and capacity to sustain research over a period of years. On the other hand, members of the Round Table were keenly aware that such large size creates both internal and external problems. Internally, the task of management becomes more difficult; externally, the public and their political representatives are suspicious of the power that is associated with such size. Consequently, the giants must be unusually well managed if they are to survive as effective, independent enterprises.

OTHER ASPECTS OF SIZE

The preceding discussion as to *why* enterprises become large naturally raised the question of *how* the growth occurred. What are the processes involved? Three suggestions were made.

The first was that growth could occur by expanding one plant. This method was used by several automobile companies in their early development, and by several steel firms. Such large concentrated plants are best suited to centralized planning, to ever more specialized staff and service units, and to the continuing oversight of a strong executive who follows personally the multitudinous activities he has helped create. This form of growth is not as popular as it once was. Except where technology dictates large concentrations of facilities, as in a complete steel plant, there is a tendency to build additions in separate locations. Improved transportation and communication facilitate this dispersion. Moreover, during the last twenty-five years there has been a sharp downward revision in what is considered the optimum manageable size.

A second way of expanding stressed by several members of the Round Table is to build (or buy) operating units in different locations. This is done even though all units do essentially the same thing and are more or less duplicates of each other. This form of growth is typical of retail chains, nation-wide drug wholesalers, large container manufacturers, dairy concerns, finance companies, and other types of business. Growth in this form raises several knotty management problems. At least a minimum of central planning and control is necessary, and usually some service operations are combined. The top executives must decide how far this central guidance and service should be carried.

The third form of growth is multiplication of product lines. More than one member of the group stressed that his company dealt with an aggregate of many kinds of products, with different characteristics, serving distinct markets. Again, management is affected. It was pointed out that thirty automobile assembly plants might be easier to manage than three divisions of a chemical firm making quite different products. Vertically integrated companies, with activities ranging from raw material processing through transportation and fabrication to consumer advertising, often face problems as divergent as the multiproduct concerns.

Members of the Round Table were alert to these various forms of expansion, but they still wanted to explore the question whether different management techniques are needed to deal with each type of growth.

Moreover, size is not only a matter of quantity—at least from the manager's point of view. One member pointed out that "manageable size" has three or more dimensions: (a) Quantity—the number of employees, the value of assets, the number of products, or the volume of sales. This is the aspect of size generally used. (b) Psychological or historical dimension. "Big" depends upon what the executives and work leaders are accustomed to. Thus, the management problems of a company which has recently trebled its size to 5,000 employees may be greater than the problems of an enterprise which has maintained a stable size of 6,000 for several years. (c) A functional dimension. An organization which includes highly specialized people, each of whom has a particular right set of answers (e.g., lawyers, accountants, engineers), is likely to encounter size difficulties even though its quantity dimensions are not great. Geographical dispersion has a similar effect.

The weaving of these different aspects of size into patterns of management will be a recurring problem in later chapters of this report.

PROBLEMS CREATED BY LARGE SIZE

Expansion from a "home town" operation of 200 or 300 employees to a 10,000-man company does indeed pose special difficulties. The management problems of the giants of 100,000 workers are even more complex. While there was no attempt to examine exhaustively the problems created by large size, members of the Round Table did testify to the following difficulties:

1. Loss of a chance for the chief executive to have face-to-face contact with the workers and first-line supervisors. It was stated that the chief executive cannot reach more than 300 to 400 people at the most, that the "human touch" is lost when the company becomes big.

2. Difficulty of getting information up and down the "line" and the necessity of formally organizing to do this. Also, there may be a breakdown of horizontal communications between units of the company which do interrelated work. Systems must be developed to supplement the normal, human contacts which are so easy in small organizations, and these systems do not always work.

3. Executive isolation. One member took the position that in large companies there is likely to be an isolated management group. This top group sees only stylized reports, staff advisers, and second or third tiers of top management. The information they receive is "screened"; in fact, their concepts and language become different from those used at the operating levels. Then communication cannot take place "no matter how warm your heart."

4. Loss of the entrepreneurial spirit. In very large organizations, do executives cease to become entrepreneurs and become bureaucrats?

5. Danger of rigidity and red tape. Order, pace, and routines are required in large organizations—and yet they

are the very stuff of red tape. Moreover, the necessary system of government may freeze into a structure of guilds or competing pressure groups.

6. The problem of determing what the top job is and how to organize for it. Some members felt that the top management job in large enterprises is sharply different from that of the head of operating divisions, and that special organization is needed to handle the top management functions. Another view was that the president should simply consider his job one of helping operating heads do their work.

7. The exercise of effective control. Since frequent personal observation of remote activities is difficult, more use is made of financial reports. But financial reports give an inadequate or tardy view of many intangibles vital to long-run success.

8. The maintenance of employee morale. The remoteness of major decisions makes it hard to give the employee any sense of participation. Company-wide systems and procedures tend to undermine employee initiative and self-reliance. "How can the employee share in the management of the corporation, and at the same time how can we have a disciplined organization that will permit fitting together all of the pieces and come out with the product the customer wants on time?"

9. Recognizing that old solutions and former ways of doing things may not fit the expanded operations. "The difficulty is to get the top management in growing companies to see what they must do to contend with size." Another member stated that he had rarely been able to

foresee what was coming and that adjustments during the growth of his concern were often forced upon him by crises of one kind or another.

METHODS OF DEALING WITH LARGE SIZE

These problems of bigness and ways of overcoming them were considered more fully in the following meetings (see Chapters 2 through 6). At the first session, two basic approaches were suggested for meeting the management problems connected with large size. Only the first approach was discussed at any length.

1. *The search for manageable units.* Several members believed that decentralization is the answer to large size. "The only problem in our company is to decentralize, to give the local manager complete authority, and to have the staff as service of the line. We feel that the nearer you can get to the simplicity of a small company, the easier it is. The problem is hard but the principle is simple."

Another member stated: "The simple way to handle bigness is to break it into manageable units. The root of the question is how do you figure out what is a manageable unit and how do you break an enterprise up into these? Is it people, diversity, markets? How do you figure out the right size and the right unit and get the right people in to run it?"

Two means of splitting into manageable units were illustrated from company experience: (a) creating individual enterprises on a product basis, (b) setting up local managers who serve a local market. Incidentally, management factors may not be the only reason for setting up small, self-contained units. In one company, for instance, product lines were split to get more concentrated sales effort. As the company grew, this separation proved to be also a great advantage in management.

A special aspect of the decentralization answer is that the chief executives need to adopt particular modes of behavior. "I make 50 plant visits per year to get to know the superintendents and the foremen and the workers who have been there for any period of time. You have to do everything you can to keep it on a small-town basis. If the top man thinks his job is to develop people as an adviser, not to act as a boss, his job can remain the same in big companies as in small plants."

Another top executive explained: "Our subsidiaries get legal and financial advice from the top staff, but that is about all. If the president of the subsidiary cannot run his business, then we replace him. We feel that we cannot put a staff in to run the business for him. A major advantage of this type of organization is that it is the best way of training an executive staff. The business is operated as a peanut stand, so to speak. The problems are essentially the same whether the business is small or large. Thus, we can transfer presidents readily and quickly from small to large firms and the man who is moved in has had a full, rounded experience."

This particular answer (decentralization) to the search for manageable units was challenged by other discussants:

"Some products are so big, turbines for example, and the customer demands all of that product from one source that you cannot decentralize to small units such as you have described."

"We have the problem of breaking a highly integrated

product into manageable hunks. This is different than operating a whole series of different businesses. In the latter case you perform as a banker and exact an accounting which may be on a very broad basis. But, in our situation, someone at the top has to fit all the pieces together. This is where the problem lies. Our top management is consumed with tremendous problems and no amount of organizing or reorganizing or sharing the load takes from the top management the basic decision such as do we build a new assembly plant or not? This decision has to be made and responsibility cannot be transferred down to the second or third tier, let alone the foreman level."

There was also some question on just how independent the local manager should be. Presumably he does not decide on capital investments; there are personnel policies he must follow; he has limitations on where he can buy; the wage rates he pays are decided for him. These are business judgments often reserved for top management, and therefore the man runs his own store or plant only on an operational basis.

From this discussion it was clear that decentralization to smaller operating units holds great promise, but special attention must be given to (a) steps and criteria to be used in establishing operating units and (b) the extent of central staff service which should be provided and the relations of this staff with the operating units.

2. *Recognition and application of principles.* A second approach to the problems of size—the recognition and application of principles—was mentioned several times during the evening. For example, one member referred to principles, saying: "A large part of our difficulty arises be-

cause we don't pay much attention to simple fundamentals such as the separation of planning, doing, and evaluating." Later, another remarked: "The principles of management are more common than the size of enterprise." The first speaker resumed: "Then you follow these simple principles: (1) confining administration to planning (which includes policy making); (2) delegating; and (3) decentralizing." It was also remarked that staff units should be regarded as service to the line and are perhaps better called service divisions.

Guides for managing large enterprises are scarce and poorly understood. Some members of the Round Table believed that great advances can be made in our thinking in this area. Others were less optimistic about the aid which principles will provide because of the varying conditions in which they will be used. Nevertheless, there was unanimous agreement that the need for skill in administering large enterprises is crucial; any further help in this area— major or minor—is well worth seeking.

2

Key Features of
Decentralization

"DECENTRALIZATION" is such an important way of dealing with large-scale operations that its use warrants careful attention. Here, as in other parts of this report, we are seeking insights on the practical application of the concept, the crucial problems which arise, the points of general agreement, and the areas in need of further study. The aim is to frame the issues.

DEFINITION

One member defined decentralization as "the complete delegation of responsibility for profit making to separate divisions of the company. Therefore, decentralization carries to each operating division authority over the primary functions which are profit making, such as, for example, engineering, production, and sales in a manufacturing organization. Divisions are judged by their resulting profits and are subject to control only to the extent that there are published, written policies."

The emphasis on local responsibility for profit making

was widely accepted. Several members were quick to say, however, that their companies were only partially decentralized—if a strict interpretation of the above definition is used.

As we shall see, in this chapter and in Chapter 7, this definition needs interpretation—perhaps qualification—when it is applied to a specific situation. Four central issues arise in almost every application:

(1) What should be the *scope* of each operating division? What does each do to make a profit?

(2) How *autonomous* should each division be? What limits or restraints on action are desirable?

(3) How *self-sufficient* should divisions be? Should service and staff activities be provided from headquarters or by each division for its own needs?

(4) What will be the *relations* between the decentralized divisions? For instance, will joint action on such things as purchasing be voluntary; and how will prices on interdivision transfer be set?

Once established, there is then the further question of how the decentralized divisions will be appraised and controlled. This topic is considered in Chapter 4.

GUIDES FOR SETTING UP DECENTRALIZED UNITS

The question of the basis on which decentralized divisions should be established was immediately raised, especially by executives whose companies are in the process of "decentralizing." Examples of the following bases were given:

Distinct product or service, e.g., division of an air conditioning company into commercial and industrial, room unit, store equipment, and associated products departments.

Geography, e.g., regional division of airlines or local stores of a department store chain.

Distinct market (type of customer or use), e.g., separation of a radio firm into home sets, government equipment, and transmitter divisions.

Not all companies are able to divide their operations neatly along some one of these lines. Several concerns find a product division works well except in sales. The same customers often buy several product lines, and a single sales force is desirable for good customer relations and for reasonably complete coverage of small accounts.

Two of the companies represented meet this difficulty by treating the selling unit as a separate operating division which works like an exclusive selling agent for several product divisions. In one case, the selling division receives a commission for its services and is expected to show a profit on its operations; the rate of commission depends upon the kind of selling service the product division requests. It was recognized that if a product division manager is *required* to sell through such a sales division, he does not have full profit-making responsibility.

Another issue in applying the above bases for decentralization is how far down to break the operations. For example, is a product division followed in *each* foreign subsidiary even though small in size? How soon are product lines large enough to be put on an independent basis? Review of just the companies represented on the Round Table revealed that some firms divide their activities into operating divisions as small as 200 or 300 employees (retail stores may be considerably smaller). Other firms stop decentralizing with divisions which have several thousand employees and are sizable undertakings by themselves.

One member said: "Unless you really believe in decentralization, you can always find an excuse for not setting up a new department. We try to break products out as soon as we know there is a definite market available. Our experience shows that the concentrated attention the new product gets when it is put on its own increases its chance of success."

Any of three factors may account for the cut-off point on decentralization. Physical technology may require a minimum size to get production efficiency. The volume needed for effective selling effort, or the instability of demand, may limit how deep decentralization is carried. A third suggested answer was that the operating units should be large enough to be able to support competent management and the necessary staff specialists, but this line is fuzzy because (as noted later) staff services may be provided by headquarters.

Once the basic operating divisions have been determined, a realistic look must be given to "full profit responsibility."

HOW "AUTONOMOUS" SHOULD DIVISIONS BE?

Even by definition, a "decentralized" division is not fully autonomous.

1. The division must conform to company *"policies."* Such policies, it was stated, are like the ground rules set up by the owner of any business. Viewed from this angle, the manager of a decentralized division may have as much

freedom of action as a separately incorporated firm. But unfortunately, as another member observed, "Policy is an elastic word. It can be a strait jacket or it can be advice." It may be used as a substitute for saying honestly that you want to "second-guess" decisions of operating divisions.

Much of the confusion about decentralization centers around the meaning attached to "policy." An example was cited of one nation-wide company which claims to be decentralized but at the same time has manuals on selling, personnel, accounting, and operations that each division manager is expected to follow and which also prepares at the home office monthly merchandising plans. Each division manager is held responsible for profitable results, to be sure, but his freedom of action is sharply restricted. This is clearly not the kind of decentralization contemplated by members of the Round Table.

"Policy" here is intended to cover general guides as to product lines, type of customers, union relations, whether to make or buy, financing of customers, and similar issues. Often the policy will be company-wide in coverage. "Detailed methods or specific procedures should not fly under the banner of 'policy' in a decentralized company." (The need for uniform accounting procedures relating to consolidated reports was recognized as a necessary exception, but such directions should not be called policies.)

In many companies the concept of policy is vague and shifting. As one member expressed it: "They use policy to mean any decision top management happens to make. It has little connection with where such decisions *should* be made, and obviously does not help the division manager know where he stands."

Two suggestions were offered for keeping "policy" from being the veiled hand which vitiates true decentralization. One is to insist that policies be put in writing and circulated to people they affect. Preferably operating executives should be consulted in the drafting of these written policies. Another approach is to make it clear that the head of a decentralized component has complete authority, except as reserved from him in writing, rather than that he has only such authority as is specifically delegated to him.

2. In addition to "policies," final decisions on certain *types of problems* are typically reserved for top management. Common restrictions on local autonomy are the following:

a. Top management should reserve the right to approve capital expenditures. Here, again, there was agreement in principle with considerable difference in application. Approval may be for a total amount or it may be for specific purposes only. One arrangement reported was an annual budget appropriation, with an understanding that the executive committee must pass upon any specific project above a certain amount. Another company is experimenting with a committee which reviews requests for capital in much the same way as a bank-loan committee would, and if the manager of the decentralized department does not make a convincing case it recommends withholding the capital. Several members expressed the view that mistakes in large capital expenditures could be so serious that "the board can't abdicate" on such matters.

b. A number of companies also require that each division prepare an operating budget. This is not for the purpose of review and approval of every item in the budget;

such control would obviously violate the principle of decentralization. Instead, top management wants to make sure that budget planning is being done and that total sales and profits are satisfactory.

c. The organization has to be planned at the top, according to one of our group. The implication was that this planning of organization should extend down into the decentralized divisions. Later, the idea was advanced that the principle of decentralization meant that the operating managers should be free to organize their respective divisions as they thought best.

d. The appointment of key personnel should be approved by top management. While this is the practice of several firms represented, one member said his company insisted only that the operating executives consider potential candidates in other divisions before making a final selection.

These are only samples of the limits placed on the autonomy of operating divisions.* The consensus of the Round Table was that the subjects and the manner of such restrictions needed a lot more study.

3. Top management also has an *intangible,* perhaps unconscious, *influence* on decentralized divisions. The attitudes, personal aims, relations with outsiders, and other ways of doing business often have a distinctly company flavor. For example, the retail stores of a large "mail-order" company—which prides itself on decentralization—have a similar atmosphere that cannot be explained solely in terms of policies and other centralized decisions.

---

* Other examples will be found in the discussion of duties of the chief executive in Chapter 3.

In firms where such strong traditions prevail, are local managers really free to act in any manner which is consistent with written policy? Or, as one member phrased it, is the climate so fixed that "thought control" results? Actions may follow customary patterns just as though a formal instruction had been issued.

The similar character of operating units was explained by one executive as follows: "We grow our managers. A fellow doesn't become manager of a division until he has eight to ten years' experience in the company. He can hire his own people, write his own ads, etc., but he naturally tends to follow the general principles of our company. He has grown up with and been inculcated with these principles. We don't think that is inconsistent with telling him he is free to make changes if he believes it is wise to do so."

This suggests a dual objective, said another member. "You are trying to do two things at once—to give the manager all the psychological satisfactions of decentralized operations, and at the same time trying to make him wise in his decisions."

Selection and training of division managers do, of course, influence the actions they will take. The crucial question is how closely they are expected to conform to their training. If each break with tradition which turns out badly is sharply criticized, then autonomy is in fact restricted. On the other hand, if differences and experimentations are not only tolerated but encouraged, the manager's independence is real.

"Decentralization" provides no easy answer to how autonomous operating divisions should be. It favors independence, but executives at all levels should be aware of the need for a nice balance between freedom and central direction.

A decision to "decentralize" still leaves a question of what central staff services should be provided for the operating divisions.

Purchasing, to obtain the benefits of mass buying, is an important example. Some companies represented insist that at least major raw materials be obtained through a central office; others make use of the buying office optional, and report that operating divisions do choose to use it; one large concern has pushed out buying to 400 locations without serious loss after the transition stage.

Legal service was also used as an illustration of the question of self-sufficiency. Here most companies favor a strong central department, but again there are exceptions.

Other central services which are important in at least some companies are *research, advertising and sales promotion, industrial relations, accounting and tax matters, pensions* and *other employee benefits, insurance, credit,* and, of course, *finance.*

Implicit in the establishment of central service departments is the idea that the quality of the services so provided will be superior to the quality of such services if they are otherwise obtained. "Our operating divisions are simply too small, and our profit margins too narrow, for us to have high grade staff in each division." Another member commented, "Duplicate staff in each unit would significantly increase our overhead."

This view was seriously challenged. "There is almost no

activity of these decentralized operations where some specialist can't show that if you let him carve that one activity out of 30 or 40 offices and plants he would make you a saving. Perhaps it's buying carbon paper or painting plants. Then you suddenly wake up and say, 'Are we in the business of buying carbon paper or painting plants or are we in the business of serving customers?' "

Several members representing multiunit companies strongly urged that central staff set up to give counsel to various operating divisions be disbanded and that this work be performed in the operating divisions themselves. Among the reasons for eliminating such staff service were the following:

(1) Central staff "service" tends to pervert the principle of decentralization. Often these units exist because the chief executive is reluctant to delegate. He wants to keep some direct strings on operations, even though the area is nominally one turned over to department heads. To the extent the chief executive does, in fact, work with and through his central staff services he is (a) upsetting the charter given to the operating departments and (b) diverting his energies from the true top management job.

(2) The expense of staff work will probably be reduced by eliminating central units. There was not full agreement on this point. Some pointed to the need for duplicate staff in each operating department. Others replied that operating heads were in a much better position to decide what service they really needed, and with profit-and-loss responsibility they would cut out unproductive work.

(3) The use of regular company-wide meetings of men

in a particular field (purchasing, industrial engineering, etc.) can provide interchange of experience and know-how without costly overhead. Personal contacts made at such meetings open the way for plant visits and informal exchange of ideas.

(4) If a special problem arises which cannot be handled by the staff within the operating department, or by contacting other departments, consultants can be used. One member stated, "As a department manager, I would rather have the opportunity to go to any of ten consulting firms than to be saddled with a person appointed by the president."

This elimination of central advisory staff is followed by companies having small as well as large operating departments. One concern with some departments of only 200–300 employees has only two nonoperating units (finance-accounting and legal) reporting to the chief executive. "The problems the central staff creates and the mistakes it brings about are more expensive than what we miss by not having the staff."

A suggestion for resolving this troublesome issue of how self-sufficient operating divisions should be was to make a careful analysis of work done by the service departments. Such analysis in one company revealed:

(1) Units doing straight operating work at the corporate level such as keeping company books or making out corporate tax returns. This is not service but plain operating. It obviously does not belong in the decentralized divisions.

(2) Units doing straight operating work such as advertising or purchasing for decentralized divisions on a contractual basis. Such units act as an outside contractor. This

work should be billed to the divisions using the service, and if the business voluntarily given to the service unit does not make it self-supporting, then the services should be bought outside. This avoids having units which are busy only part time dreaming up activities to justify their existence. If only one or two divisions use the service, the unit should be transferred to them.

(3) Units doing legitimate staff work keeping up with trends inside and outside the company in a given functional or subfunctional area and trying to see that the knowledge they gain is made available to all the operating units. This work may be dispersed to the operating divisions, as suggested earlier. Or, central units may be retained for reasons of economy, to assure adequate attention, or to provide necessary counsel to top management as well as to the divisions.

From the viewpoint of responsibility, costs of the corporate-wide work should not be charged to the operating divisions since they have no control. Several firms do make assessments, however, so that these costs will be considered in setting prices and in thinking about profits.

The broad issue of self-sufficiency of decentralized divisions probably has been given even less thought than questions of autonomy. Individual services (law, personnel, purchasing, etc.) have been discussed at length, but rarely in terms of an over-all pattern. The clash of views indicated above clearly shows that this is another area needing careful study.

RELATIONS BETWEEN DECENTRALIZED DIVISIONS

Complete "decentralization" still leaves some questions about the relations between the operating divisions.

A common problem is the price at which goods are transferred between divisions. A manufacturing department may sell to a general sales department, or one product division may sell its product to another product division. Should these transfers be made at cost or on a full-price basis?

The practice of one company was described as follows: "We put a profit yardstick on both the manufacturing and sales components. We treat the sales component as the customer of the manufacturing component and as a profit-making business like a jobber." The bargaining here is done at arm's length and if the divisions cannot agree on a price they are free to go outside. This sort of arrangement is fully consistent with decentralization. The freedom of action and the responsibility of the operating divisions are not impaired.

In other companies where divisions are *required* to deal with each other, a fair price may be hard to agree upon. Rarely are strictly comparable prices available from a competitive market, so negotiation is necessary. Supplying divisions may become overly complacent about efficiency if they have an assured sale; there is no clear way to allocate any savings that result from the direct dealing. Profit and cost information in addition to that available to outside competitors is sometimes given to other divisions to serve as a basis of agreement. Such information is not always helpful, however, since the less profitable division naturally seeks a price adjustment; this tends to conceal efficiencies and inefficiencies.

Because of the unsatisfactory nature of negotiated prices for intercompany transfers, several of the firms represented at the Round Table reported that they shift goods at standard costs. This has the advantage of showing final profits only in one place. Such a practice is more likely to be followed in highly integrated firms where there is little opportunity for operating divisions to buy and sell on the outside as well as internally.

These questions of the basis of interdivision transfers are not created by decentralization. They exist under any management philosophy. Decentralization does bring them to the surface, however, because of the increased pressure on each division to show good results. The fullest benefits arise when each division can be independent in its actions.

A second type of relationship between decentralized divisions is that of obtaining interdivisional coordination on special problems, such as competing for a limited supply of raw material. This is a tricky problem for decentralized companies to handle if they wish to stick to the autonomy principle. As one member indicated: "A peculiar shortage was taken care of by calling the local purchasing agents together and saying, 'You are all in this together and it looks like you are acting as fools. Now you're all in the same outfit and we're not going to tell you what to do unless you force us to. You get around the table yourselves and decide what is the sensible thing to do and you do it.' "

Also, a number of members felt that on some matters, such as advertising copy, public relations, or employee benefits, the actions of the several operating divisions should be uniform or at least consistent. "The answer is here that you can't have real decentralization and consistency."

Not all companies can go the whole way with decentralization. As noted in Chapter 1, the very reason for their growth may preclude giving operating divisions the degree of independence suggested above. Integrated enterprises such as automobile manufacturers, for instance, must achieve close sychronization on design, quality, and schedules. We will return to the problems of these concerns in the final chapter of this report.

The concept of decentralization is nonetheless clear. It is really a philosophy of management. For large and ever growing enterprises it offers probably the best way known to meet the problems of bigness.

The application of the decentralization philosophy is no easy task. Among the issues to be resolved are (a) the scope of each operating division, (b) the degree of autonomy to be granted, (c) the extent to which the divisions will be self-contained, and (d) the relations between divisions. These issues have been reviewed in this chapter. Other questions, such as what role the chief executive should perform and how control should be obtained, are examined in remaining chapters of this report.

3

Job of the Chief Executive

HAVING CONSIDERED "operating divisions" in the preceding chapter, we may now center our attention on the job of top management.

In large and expanding enterprises, what should the president do? This question was of special interest to members of the Round Table since most of them held top management positions. Their views and insights focused on the following areas:

(a) What are the duties of the chief executive? How should he utilize his time and energies?

(b) What organizational schemes are needed for the top management job?

(c) How does the job change with changing size of the enterprise?

(d) Does the kind of man needed change with changing size of the enterprise?

The president of a medium-sized or small company is also concerned with similar questions. He may not be able to devote his time exclusively to top management duties, but he is nonetheless responsible for making sure that the chief executive functions are well performed in his firm.

DUTIES OF THE CHIEF EXECUTIVE

The broad outlines of the chief executive's job are easier to define than the specific details. There was general agreement that the head of a company should:

1. *Plan.* This includes setting objectives, determining policies, devising strategies—especially on a long-range basis.
2. *Administer.* The chief executive must select key personnel, coordinate, control, and provide leadership.
3. *Perform Other Duties.* Public appearances, contacts with government and industry executives, and other company representation are inescapable.

The demands on the limited time of a top executive are great, and he must carefully consider how he can best perform the above duties. There appears to be wide difference in practice, as will be indicated in the analysis of each general function.

PLANNING

At the head of the list of top management duties is planning. As one member said: "The primary duty of the president is to set objectives and to make basic decisions on how to reach these objectives." Another seasoned executive observed: "First it is strategy. What is this company going to do? He must work out the vision of what the objective is going to be."

In a container company, for example, the president had to decide whether printing on tin plate would be done at the mills where the plate was purchased or at the can plants. Economies could be obtained by having the work done at the supplier's mills, but the president decided against this plan because it would have made the company more vulnerable to strikes and other interruptions. Flexibility had to be balanced against cost.

Several executives testified that they spent considerable time deciding on products to be added to their line; and, if the addition was desirable, whether to expand an existing plant, build a new one, or buy another company.

Long-term commitments such as leases or dealer franchises often receive top-side attention. Also, the president of one company took on himself the resolution of a question whether to use one or several suppliers of a major material. Other examples of top management planning include decisions on large investments and mechanization. Two members said their companies were forced by outside conditions to negotiate with a union on a company-wide basis.

These examples are suggestive, but they may not fit another situation. The chief executive of an expanding firm needs more explicit guides for the planning he should do. Several suggestions were made.

1. Emphasis should be on *long-range* plans. One executive stated that "the most important task of the president is to decide what the company is going to be doing five years from now." Other members affirmed the need for looking years ahead of current operations and considering in what directions the efforts of the enterprise should be turned.

A large automobile manufacturer is in difficulty because its long-range planning was faulty. Fifteen years ago this firm took the position that sales were the heart of its business and that production should be kept as simple as possible. In line with this thinking, it followed a deliberate policy of farming out everything except engine making and assembly. This has proven to be unwise, and the firm is now having difficulties assimilating body and parts production. A member of our group summarized the situation: "They were so busy operating the type of business they knew that they missed the trend of the industry. They forgot to project themselves into the future where their business lay."

2. Whenever possible decisions should be in terms of *patterns* rather than single problems. Objectives, policies, and even lists of crucial factors provide continuing guidance. By framing decisions in this way "the top manager acts as a fire prevention officer rather than as someone who is putting out fires all the time."

The chief executive of one very large enterprise, for example, will make decisions only on subjects that can be stated in terms of company policy. Unless and until a policy has been written out, discussed with the operating men affected, and approved by the chief executive, authority and responsibility are decentralized. One instance was cited in which operating executives had to make agreements involving up to fifty million dollars each. A year and a half later, after considerable experience had been gained, a policy was formulated, but in the interim top management refused to make decisions on single transactions.

A number of our group felt that this was carrying decentralization too far, that the company then became little more than an investment trust, that top management was abdicating its responsibilities. To be sure, the formulation of policy is desirable, but it was stated that there are a variety of additional decisions which should be made from a company-wide point of view.

In following the pattern type of decision making, there are at least two questions which the chief executive needs to ask about issues he undertakes: "(1) Is this covered by an existing policy? If so, I can and should return the problem to operating executives. (2) If the issue is not covered by existing policy, then is this general enough so that I should establish a new policy to deal with it?" Through such an approach, the executive is continually reducing the number of specific issues that need to come to his attention.

3. There should be an understanding of what problems the chief executive *will not decide.* This goes back to decentralization and a determination to make it work. "One of the hardest things I had to learn," said a senior executive, "was to stop making decisions that belong to my former job and give my full attention to problems of the new job—knowing that I was still responsible for results."

Clearly "the chief executive should not make decisions which are entirely within the purview of a subordinate." Also, as already suggested, he should not deal with matters already covered by policy. At least he should make it clear that the argument for an exception will have to be very strong before he will become involved.

Such practice helps to keep the top executive out of details, but to one member at least, "it really begs the question of what should be delegated and what reserved." Another member suggested three criteria of where decisions belong: "(a) futurity—the time for which you make a decision and the speed with which you may have to reverse it, (b) impact outside its own area—its company-wide nature, and (c) number of qualitative considerations involved—judgments involving human beings, morale, public reaction, and the like." These were advanced as guides for developing a "common law" of what kind of problems to take to the top boss.

ADMINISTERING

The head of a company must get things done, as well as plan. He probably spends a smaller part of his day on this "execution of plans" than do his managers and superintendents; nevertheless, it is an essential part of his job.

Picking key men as associates and assistants was given top priority by members of the Round Table. Nothing is more crucial to success, nor can this duty be evaded.

Along with selection goes aid in personal development. The men surrounding a chief executive will normally be very competent individuals. Still, the top men can often increase the usefulness of such individuals through assignments that have training value, through coaching, and by other means.*

Executive personnel duties also include the obligation to remove men (through transfer if not dismissal) whose work is unsatisfactory. The larger the company, and the greater the decentralization, the more important it is to have the right men in key posts. This means that the chief

* Executive personnel problems were explored more fully in another series of round table meetings. See Eli Ginzburg, *What Makes an Executive? Report of a Round Table on Executive Potential and Performance* (Columbia University Press, 1955).

executive must maintain an objectivity and strength of character about moving men who are likely to be personal friends as well as company manpower. Some members of the Round Table, though not all, felt that the chief executive had to be somewhat aloof in order to perform his personnel duties properly.

The president has still another personnel duty, which is to listen to members of his organization who have personal problems arising from their association with the organization. "Any man in the company has the right of appeal if he feels that he is underpaid, passed up on promotion, or otherwise unfairly treated." ". . . the president will be swamped with such cases unless he insists that all intermediate levels of supervision be consulted before a man comes to him. Also corrective action, if any, should be taken through the channel of command."

Closely related to the choice of executive personnel is the duty to *build and maintain a sound organization structure.* Setting up manageable divisions and placing staff in strategic spots are steps in building the structure, as pointed out in the preceding chapter. A more delicate but no less vital phase is clarifying relationships. One member insisted: "The no-man's land of organization is relationships. We have given far too little thought to how people can work together best."

Maintaining the organization structure requires self-discipline on the part of top management. It was repeatedly stated that, while communication through informal channels is desirable, the chief executive must insist that decisions be made within the framework of the formal organization. "The general never talks officially to a major, although, in a friendly way, he will talk to a sergeant."

This practice of sticking to formal channels is necessary (1) to avoid an unmanageable number of problems coming to the chief executive and (2) to build up the operating executives who are designated to resolve such issues.

Moreover, the chief executive himself is expected to limit his decision making to conform strictly to the pattern of delegation of responsibility he has established. The concept of letting the divisional vice-presidents work out their own problems was advanced as a principle of management. "The subordinate must come to him with a decision, not for a decision." "The man down the line will make the decision clean if he knows he is going to be hung with it, and he won't make it as clean if he can say to himself: 'Well, it really doesn't make any difference, the president will take the rap anyway.'"

Another major administrative task is *coordination.* Interdivisional problems occupy some of the time of every chief executive. Relations between a captive mill and three processing divisions using the raw material, for example, require top management attention in one concern especially when supply is short. Another member of the group remarked that in his company conflicts, such as which division was to handle the development of a particular product, had to be arbitrated frequently. "I try to dispose of them promptly, on a day-to-day basis if I can."

Two approaches to the coordinative element of the top management job were described. One chief executive asks for definite recommendations from the operating or staff divisions concerned and uses these as the basis for the ultimate decision. This particular executive hears about such problems once each month at a scheduled meeting of his chief subordinates and spends the next month working them out.

In another company, coordination is the primary responsibility of the operating executives themselves. First emphasis is placed upon their getting together to solve mutual problems without being asked to do so. Problems that cannot be settled on this basis will be brought up to the chief executive, although not at a formal meeting. Thus, there appears to be considerable difference in the way the problems requiring coordination are initially approached and also in the organizational devices used to reconcile such problems.

Leadership is also vital. A member suggested that in the administrative aspects of the top management job, in contrast to the planning function, the primary job is one of leadership. This was rephrased by another speaker who said, "The chief executive in a company like our own is responsible for the team and the way the team plays." The leadership task appears to be of critical importance when coordination is also involved. For example, it was said that "our past president was a master at reconciling opinions and guiding a group to sound decisions. However, there was never any question as to where the head of the table was."

Exercise of the function of leadership appears to be closely related to the size of the company. For example, the question was raised about dealing with the able individual who got along poorly with the other executives.

One member stated that the president could not afford to concern himself with smoothing out the relations "because he would then be just a mopper-upper" and would not fulfill his duty of staying out of current operations and concerning himself with future plans. Another member held that "the bigger the company gets, the less time the president has to smooth things and the more carefully he has to pick the men. Only in a smaller company can he take on the mediation problem."

The use of command and the use of persuasion were discussed in relation to the size of the enterprise. One speaker held that leadership by persuasion is much more a requisite in big companies than in little ones, if only for the reason that people of wider experience are being dealt with. To the statement that some complex situations require quick action which precludes the persuasive process, the reply was made that large companies should have foreseen these occurrences and from past experience have developed check lists to aid in action. This tends to make command by top management unnecessary.*

The last administrative task singled out was *control.* Whether plans be stated only as general objectives or be reduced to specific budget estimates, the chief executive must take steps to assure that performance is in line with plans. Profits, return on investment, interdivisional comparisons, market position, and variations from budgets were suggested as useful criteria.

* These observations on leadership and command raise some interesting corollary questions. Does persuasive leadership rely on accurate forecasting, and thus run the risk of inflexibility when operating conditions change unexpectedly? Are there reasons why a smaller company cannot, and should not, rely on persuasive leadership just as much as a large company?

Control, especially in a large enterprise, is a tricky activity. It was the topic of an entire evening's discussion, and is reviewed more fully in Chapter 4.

The time a chief executive devotes to each of these elements of administering—executive personnel, organization structure, coordination, leadership, and control—varies widely from one situation to the next. In total, however, they place heavy burdens on his energies.

OTHER DUTIES

The top management job involves duties besides those connected with planning and administering. A major one of these is the ceremonial task. Several speakers indicated that a president spends a lot of time shaking hands and awarding service pins. Much of this task cannot be delegated to a subordinate but has to be performed by the chief officer himself. Similarly, one member stated that a duty of the president is to see every plant at least once a year. This is in part for control purposes but also for the purpose of showing himself to the members of the organization.

The ceremonial task includes contacts not only with members of the company but with many outside organizations. The chief executive must spend time with investment analysts, government committees, trade associations, customers, and people seeking charitable contributions. The pressure on the chief executive to take part in outside activities tends to increase with the size of the company, and care is required in limiting time used for such purposes without hurting public relations. Several of the group stressed, however, that these outside contacts often were useful sources of information. "If you keep your ears open and ask questions, you can learn a lot from people who are not inside the company."

The amount of time spent with customers, trade associations, and charitable groups appears to vary with the willingness of the top management to make the decisions in which these groups are interested. For example, some members of the Round Table have found that very little of their time is occupied in dealing with investment analysts. "I tell them to see the Treasurer." Others will take all the time such investigators ask for and feel that it is time well spent because of the analysts' objective view and fund of information.

The question of charitable contributions often is passed down to operating executives as close to the local level as possible. Adherence to this principle, it was stated, helps to relieve the chief executive from being placed on committees to obtain charitable contributions.

Also important in other duties of a chief executive is work on special problems. These naturally vary from time to time. One month it may be a company-wide strike, and the next it may be taxes. Some top executives are active in negotiations for purchase of new companies, patents, or raw material sources. New financing may call for attention. Or, pending legislation may be so important that the president "lives in Washington for a month."

Special problems there will be, even though just what they will involve cannot be forecast. Consequently, Round Table members urged that the chief executive keep himself free of routine so that he will be able to tackle the unusual problems as they arise.

ORGANIZATION FOR THE TOP MANAGEMENT JOB

The burdens on the top executive in any large enterprise are heavy and inescapable. Decentralization may make the job doable, but by no means simple. As already noted, there will always remain a need for (a) broad and long-range planning, (b) selecting key men, organizing and coordinating their efforts, and providing leadership, and (c) personally attending innumerable meetings and ceremonies—and at the same time having free time to work on sudden problems.

Four approaches to organizing the work of top management were reported in the Round Table. For want of better terms, these may be called:

(1) group responsibility
(2) use of operating executives on the top management team
(3) use of staff
(4) separation of planning and administering

Group responsibility. Several members of our group challenged the concept of a single chief executive. One man who is familiar with many companies felt that often two men, or in large concerns three men, really shared the job. The titles might differ but the idea was that the organizational status of the men was about the same and that all three participated in essential decisions. Another speaker agreed that in his company there were three chief subordinates "who were practically on a level" with the president. The question was raised as to whether there was, then, *a* chief executive or a group performing the top management duties.

Still another participant explained that his company relied upon an executive committee to do the top management job. Each member of the committee is in charge of several operating divisions. It is also the duty of each member to keep in close and frequent contact with other members of the executive committee. This close association provides opportunity for mutual advice and for co-ordination where necessary.

Each operating division prepares a budget, and these budgets are presented separately and in consolidated form to the executive committee. The monthly review of these budgets and of actual results enables the committee to see the financial picture of the entire company. It is then in a position to decide on the soundness, from an over-all viewpoint, of expansion into a new line and similar major issues.

In effect, then, this company uses a full-time executive committee to expand the capacity of the chief executive. (This arrangement is similar to a small, full-time board of directors each member of which devotes his time exclusively to top management duties.)

Objection was immediately raised that formal organization requires a *single* person who is responsible to the board. There was general agreement that one man must take final responsibility and that formal recognition should not be given to any other device for delegating the top authority and responsibility.

At the same time there was testimony that, in fact, several men may work closely together in running the company. The question of who has the final "say" is rarely raised. Instead, each man has a keen sense of obligation for the entire operation. By mutual consent the work is divided up, but all important decisions have the endorsement of the group as a whole. Within the group, deference to knowledge and experience is far more significant than formal authority. Formal authority is treated largely as a safety valve to be used only if group action breaks down.

Management team. A different arrangement is the use of key operating subordinates as members of the top management team. Here the second echelon of a company serves in both operating and top management capacities.

One speaker said that this could occur in his company because the divisions did not compete but were complementary. Another stated that formal recognition has been given in his company to the device of the "executive office." The vice-presidents who are members of this office (along with the president) are expected to run their own divisions part of the time but also to spend a specified part of their time "looking at problems the way the president does, acting and thinking as the president."

In its more advanced form the management team may also be the board of directors. While one member stated that he had had no experience with such a board and did not believe that an "inside" board could perform the same role as an "outside" board, other members indicated that "inside" boards are used in their companies. Resolution of the seeming conflict of authority between the president and the men who are his subordinates at one time and equals at another, it was explained, may be achieved in two ways: (a) through effective exercise of leadership and (b) through the type of decisions brought to the board. One speaker said, "In my case I don't feel that having the vice-presidents sit on the board affects my authority." Another stated, "We simply don't take operating decisions to the board."

An important advantage of this management team approach is that a gulf between top and operating management is virtually impossible. On the other hand, it calls for able and versatile executives, and even then there is danger that short-run operating problems will steal time which should be devoted to top management problems. Also, a management team is more effective in the planning aspects of top management work than in administering and "other duties."

Staff as an aid to top management. Most large companies have at least some staff in "the office" of the chief executive to help him perform his duties. However, our discussion indicated considerable difference in the work done in this "office." The basic issue affecting the work of such staff is what authority the chief executive reserves and what he turns over to the operating departments. Even assuming—as we did—a high degree of decentralization, there is no clear-cut role for top management staff.

The amount and nature of central staff work depends primarily upon the concept of the work the chief executive should do. Central administration of a union contract or review of capital expenditures calls for one type of staff. Long-range planning and policy formulation calls for another. Negotiation of financial deals is still a different matter. Keeping the chief executive posted and prepared for ceremonials, congressional hearings, and other public contacts is also a specialized sort of job.

Organization for the top management job may also include specialists in the interpretation and presentation of figures on behalf of the "executive office." These men are occupied with carrying out part of the control function. One speaker stated that in his organization there are two men who reported specifically to the president for the purpose of interpreting all figures from every source. Others took sharp exception to a control group (as developed in the Army Services of Supply) in addition to a "company controller."

Caution against building up large central staffs was advised. There is danger that such a staff will usurp duties which can be done better in operating divisions or by senior executives themselves. Nevertheless, most companies will need at least some staff that can "afford the luxury of a company-wide point of view." Sound plans for the size and nature of this remaining staff group, however, must be built on a clearer concept of the top management job than we now have.

Separation of planning and administering. Still another suggestion for organizing top management work is to draw a rather sharp distinction between planning tasks and administrative tasks, and assign these to separate men. The titles of the two men may be Chairman of the Board, and President; President, and Executive Vice-President; or President, and General Manager.

With increasing size a greater proportion of the time of the top executive needs to be devoted to planning and studying the problem of over-all design of the enterprise and a lesser proportion to operations. The planning tasks soon make up a full-time job and eventually require the efforts of more than one person. One speaker urged that it was necessary to distinguish early between execution and planning and to define the jobs. "Either job is full time in even a moderate sized company. The chief executive is the man doing the directing, coordinating, and decision making for men reporting to him every day. He cannot mix it with broad planning. The top planner is a man who keeps his time free for thinking ahead."

The practicality of this more conventional approach was challenged. "The so-called planning job is too often given to a man who should have been retired." Again, "The man who has been an operating executive all of his life doesn't become a planner just because his title has been changed to Chairman of the Board." In other words, the prestige attached to particular positions may interfere with the selection of men best qualified to do the assigned duties.

One member of the Round Table goes even further. He grants that the four approaches to top management organization—group responsibility, operating men on the top management team, use of staff, and separation of planning and administering—are suggestive. But, the personality of the president and the relationships between the men around him are crucial. The choice of any one of the four approaches, or a combination of them, he feels, must be adapted to the key people. The important thing is to recognize the top management tasks and be sure they get done well.

DISTINGUISHING CHARACTERISTICS OF THE TOP MANAGEMENT
JOB IN LARGE AND SMALL ENTERPRISES

Differences in the nature and organization of the chief executive's work are, of course, due to many factors. The personality of the man, traditions of the company, the technological and competitive nature of the industry, all affect the top management set-up. Size, too, is a factor. Although we did not attempt to reach agreement on the following, these points regarding the effect of size were raised during the course of our discussion:

1. As the enterprise grows, planning must be done increasingly in terms of patterns (objectives, principles, policies, standing procedures, guides for analysis) and less on a single situation basis.

2. In this connection, the scope of "policy" tends to change with size. Problems which are unusual in small companies may occur often enough in large firms to be covered by a policy. Likewise, "what is called policy in a small company becomes routine in a large one."

3. This shifting nature of policy makes decentralization (i.e., "full profit-making responsibility within company *policy*") a slippery concept, especially in large companies. One multiproduct concern deliberately sets up company policies only where the over-all interest is common.

4. As size increases the chief executive must spend more of his time on planning and can give less attention to administration. There is less time for arbitration of differences, detail control, and seeing that the team plays together.

5. Moreover, as companies grow, planning by the chief

executive deals more and more with long-range problems and less with current issues. "If you mix today's and next year's work, today's work will draw all the time."

6. The bigger the company, the more need there is for several men to share in the work of the chief executive. A full-time chairman as well as a president, a "president's office," staff assistants to the president, and specific recognition that vice-presidents are to devote at least part of their time to the job of the president are among the organization devices used to assure that the chief executive's duties are performed well.

DOES SIZE AFFECT THE KIND OF MAN NEEDED
AS CHIEF EXECUTIVE?

The changing nature of the top management job with a change in size requires a shift in attitude toward the duties and a conscious awareness of the necessity for this change in attitude. One member stated that many presidents will not decide what they are going to do with their time or what kind of decisions they will and will not make. Other speakers felt that the "will not" was most important; that the chief executive's function was to be available, not involved in details; and that he must forget the types of problems with which he was formerly concerned.

In other words, increasing size changes the qualities which are most needed for the top executive job. "In larger and more complex places the doer can't live. It takes the man who will plan and think and put time limits on himself."

This shift in the kind of man needed may be considerable, but it seems to be not so imposing as the change required in moving from managing a particular department to a top management job. The question was asked: "What do you do when the sales manager becomes president? He has a completely different job with different work content and a different mental process." A member replied: "This is the biggest argument for autonomous units in decentralization. You force the sales manager into changing his spots while he is still young enough to do it and while his operation is still small enough to prevent mistakes from being catastrophic."

The foregoing distillation of ideas coming out of the Round Table discussions gives no simple, sharp definition of the job of the chief executive. Nevertheless, out of the experience of the group does emerge an array of concepts and suggestions. These can be useful as guides to the executive trying to think through a workable plan for the top job in his particular company.

4

Appraising Results of Operations

THE DELEGATION of authority, which is vital in the effective
operation of large-scale enterprises, creates the need for
some sort of measurement and evaluation of performance.
Final responsibility continues to rest on top management,
and this makes proper evaluation of the work of subordinates an essential process. Without such discerning
appraisal of past results, the chief executive lacks a sound
basis for future planning, for decisions regarding executive
personnel, and for other duties discussed in Chapter 3.

Our discussion of this evaluation process may be summarized under the following headings:

1. Who or what is being measured?
2. What criteria should be applied to operating departments?
3. What criteria are useful in judging service divisions?
4. How should top executives get information on actual
operations? How are the criteria applied?

WHO OR WHAT IS BEING MEASURED?

One member immediately asked whether we should try
to appraise the collective performance of a department or
a division, or the performance of the individual who heads

the unit. Under some circumstances, executive performance might be good even though his departmental results
were considered to be poor, or vice versa. For instance,
severe competition or difficulties inherited from the preceding manager may cause poor results for a time—even
with the best of management.

During the evening, three broad ways of dealing with
this question were proposed:

(a) Over-all criteria of departmental performance may
be established, e.g., return on investment, and both the
department and its top executive judged in terms of these
criteria. The usefulness of this approach is improved if the
level of attainment—par for the course—is adjusted from
time to time in light of current objectives and operating
difficulties.

(b) A series of more detailed operating standards may
be used to appraise departmental performance and also
executive achievement. Here a variety of gauges are possible, such as production costs, machine outputs, employee
or inventory turnover, etc. Companies with several comparable plants, branches, or stores often use this approach;
and a few industries have trade associations which develop
helpful standards of this type. If this approach is carried
very far it tends to undermine full decentralization.

(c) Instead of judging an executive by the general or
specific results of his department, as outlined in (a) and
(b), emphasis may be placed on *how* he does his work.
How does he size up competition; how does he think; how
energetic is he in correcting weak spots; how does he treat
his men, etc.? Unfortunately, there is no "one best way"
for an executive to act, so this type of standard is difficult

to apply. Nevertheless, it probably has a significant bearing on most subjective appraisals of individual executives, and is especially pertinent for men doing staff or service work where results are hard to measure—as in the case of purchasing or legal work. Here attention is clearly shifted from the department to the individual.

Although we did not pursue this topic fully, the implications of other discussion were that much more needs to be learned about methods of management before we can effectively measure executive work per se. For managers of operating departments, at least, it is simpler and probably better to identify individual performance with the suc-- cess of the department—*provided* the departmental criteria include intangible and long-range factors and are adjusted to current conditions.

CRITERIA FOR JUDGING OPERATING DIVISIONS

Return on investment is probably the most widely used measure of performance for decentralized departments. Such departments have "profit-and-loss responsibility," so this is a natural standard. As developed by du Pont, this concept also includes other basic financial ratios such as earnings on sales and turnover of investment.

"You can't judge effectiveness except by return on investment. If you have bad labor relations, it will affect return on investment. If you let inventories get out of hand or employ excessive amounts of capital for any other reason, it will have the same result."

Virtually all of the companies represented in our group watch these financial ratios, but there was considerable difference of opinion regarding their adequacy.

The simple use of "return on investment" was questioned: "Is immediate profit the prime consideration, or should that be sacrificed for volume? It's long-range profits as well as next year's that you have to think about."

A more flexible standard described by one member consists of carefully prepared annual forecasts which are translated into *budgets* for each operating department. These forecasts and budgets, drawn up initially by the departments themselves, are reviewed by an executive committee with special emphasis on business outlook, industry competition, and similar factors. This process introduces considerable personal judgment into the targets set but gives a definite financial standard which may be compared with actual results each month.

Complete or even primary reliance upon conventional accounting figures, as provided in the two preceding suggestions, was challenged several times during the evening. One member noted that the annual profit standard encourages operating managers to take a short-run view—to the detriment of such important things as research, maintenance, public relations, and executive development. Another participant explained that in the automobile industry many of the expenses for engineering, design, dealer organization, and the like do not yield profits until several years after they are incurred. By cutting down on such expense "we might live on fat for five years, showing a nice profit, but leave the business a shambles."

"I am as skeptical of any *one* standard as I am of an airplane which has only an altimeter. The problem is to make management aware of the many intangible factors affecting profit and of the need for balance of two time dimensions—the immediate and the long-range."

Again, "The fetish of attempting to measure management effectiveness by formula has taken hold of industry to the point where I think it has lost contact with reality. . . . There is an area of subjective evaluation that has to be applied. This is the next major question of measurement that modern business has to face up to."

The limitations of conventional accounting reports as measures of operating results, which were emphasized in the discussion, were of two types. (a) The accounting cycle of one year, along with arbitrary rules as to what must be treated as expense and income within that period, is too short a time to show the results of many managerial actions. "The accounting year is one of management's unnecessary tyrannies." (b) Several vital aspects of successful operations are either never shown directly in the accounts, or are misleadingly recorded since their value is not proportional to cash outlays. Company position in the industry or favorable union relations, for instance, do not show on the books. Eventually, of course, these unrecognized assets and liabilities will be reflected in the profit account, but not in a way that can be ascribed to a particular management.

Consequently, most of our group felt that *additional criteria* are essential for an adequate appraisal of operating departments. Comparison of company sales and profits to those of other companies in its industry was suggested several times. One company develops a measure of "market fertility" (potential) for each of its products and gauges actual sales against this standard.

A *comprehensive list* of criteria, which embraces most of the other suggestions, was presented by one of the group:

1. Profitability—in both percent of sales and return on investment
2. Market position
3. Productivity—which means improving costs as well as sales
4. Leadership in technological research
5. Development of future people, both technical or functional and managerial
6. Employee attitudes and relations
7. Public attitudes
8. Balance of long- and short-range objectives

The list was recognized as needing further definition of subfactors, adaptation to specified operations, and other refinements. Nevertheless, it does provide comprehensive coverage within a manageable number of factors.

In the discussion of this multiple factor approach to management appraisal, there was stress on the need to *vary the weights* according to the particular situation. Thus, product research in 1955 should be given much more weight in a company or department producing hormones than one producing, say, quinine where the growth prospects are much more modest.

It was recommended that the weights assigned to factors should be adjusted to the objectives set by top management for a given operating department. In this way, the targets can be spread over a period of years in a realistic and strategic way. Some departments, for example, may concentrate on market penetration for several years, while others may seek a high return on established reputation.

Several specific instances of shifts in objectives were

reported. A large lumber company has recently sub-
ordinated almost all other objectives to that of timber
land development; at present rates of industry and company cutting, the facilities of the company will be almost
useless in twenty years unless the timber resource problem
is solved. Another firm, by contrast, has been short of
capital and during the last three years has knowingly
stressed current profits at the expense of dealer good-will
and product improvement. In still another case, a decentralized division of a large oil company did not take full
advantage of its transportation situation—at the sacrifice
of several million dollars in profit—because of the likely
effect such action would have had on suppliers serving
other divisions of the company.

With a shift in relative importance of objectives, such
as those just noted, there naturally should be a corre-
sponding change in the standards used to measure managerial performance. To achieve desired results, first, all
men directly concerned—top management, division
management, and key staff—must have a mutual understanding on what weights to give the various objectives;
and, second, the results should be judged according to
this same set of values.

In addition to the need for more study of the selection
and weighting of appraisal factors, three drawbacks were
noted:

(1) There is danger that the approach will be reduced
to a formula, and several of our group doubted if
any formula would be flexible enough to fit all
situations.

(2) Stockholders are accustomed to thinking in terms

of financial results only, and an educational job must be done to get them to accept these more comprehensive management standards. It was noted, however, that companies with several operating units might avoid such stockholder complaint if some units showed enough profits in a given year to "carry" the other units where stress was being laid on long-run or intangible accomplishments.

(3) Several of the criteria in the comprehensive list pose difficult measurement problems. Subjective judgments are involved, and these open the way for clashes of opinion between top management and operating executives. We will return to these problems of measurement later in this chapter.

CRITERIA FOR JUDGING SERVICE DIVISIONS

The task of evaluating the performance of service and staff divisions was recognized as even more difficult than judging decentralized operating units. The output of such divisions is largely intangible, and this leads to difficulties in comparing costs with results.

Two basic questions, members of the Round Table insisted, should be asked whenever auxiliary divisions are being appraised: (1) What work should each division do? (2) How well and how efficiently is this work being performed?

Several instances of failure to ask "what work should be done?" were reported. As a result, emphasis had been placed on being highly expert in, say, patent work or costs-per-mile without appraising the value of that work to the enterprise. In the transportation example, much more money was saved by eliminating truck miles entirely than by detailed analysis of truck operation. A first step, then, in evaluating an auxiliary division is to consider its "contribution to the business as a whole."

One member explained that his company has a "patent committee"—with representatives from the sales, production, research, and legal departments—which decides what patent action is important to pursue. (The committee is not concerned with efficiency of the patent lawyers.) This arrangement emphasizes the need for broad judgment and an over-all viewpoint in evaluating the output of an auxiliary division. It is akin to setting the relative weights on criteria used to judge operating departments. What are your objectives; what do you want done?

The second basic question is "How effectively and how efficiently is the division doing its assigned work?" Occasionally competitive standards are available. The service and costs of the printing division may be compared with those of outside firms. To a lesser extent, the operations of a legal department may be contrasted with the use of independent counsel. But these are rough standards at best, and become increasingly difficult to use for service activities which are closely interwoven with other company activities. Most accounting or personnel work, for example, cannot be subcontracted.

Intercompany comparisons are of doubtful value because of differences in work performed and in organization.

Here, again, the criteria often shift from results to *how* the work is being done (as explained in point (c) on page 59). Do the men in the department appear to be working effectively, i.e., "playing a good game"? Tradition and subjective impressions inevitably play an important part in this type of appraisal. Or, as two of our group said, you hire an expert in whom you have confidence and simply rely on him to run his division well.

Because of the continuing need to be sure that work of auxiliary divisions does contribute to primary operations, and because of the difficulty in setting standards of service and cost, it was urged that the organization of service and staff work be kept close to operating departments. The larger the company the more important this becomes. "A functional manager who is more than one level away from the operation he serves begins to be a professor —more interested in his specialty than in results."

GETTING INFORMATION ON ACTUAL PERFORMANCE

Standards are useful only as we are able to compare them with actual performance. The management standards already suggested include such criteria as improved technology, executive development, and public relations. And, where the accomplishment itself defies reliable measurement, an appraisal of *how* the work is being done was recommended. Judging actual performance in such terms poses real problems.

Members of the Round Table testified to the skill and judgment needed in keeping adequately informed. Decentralization removes the chief executive from close contact with daily operations. Moreover, there is a natural tendency to report the good and conceal the bad; two or three such screenings of facts done successively produce a distorted picture. The result is executive isolation.

Executive isolation is not entirely bad. "If you try to get too much information up to the one man at the lofty pinnacle, he is going to have a feeling that he knows a lot more than he does. He will therefore make dangerous decisions. The chief executive should only get the kind of facts needed to do top management work." But top management must not be too isolated. Assuming the criteria already discussed are necessary to judge operating divisions properly, then reliable data in these areas should be obtained.

Accounting reports on sales, expenses, earnings, uses of capital, turnovers, return on investment, and the like will, of course, be used. Also statistical data showing relative market position and relation of company operations to economic conditions are usually helpful.

However, the inadequacy of conventional accounting reports for appraising subordinates has already been noted. Accounting figures should be used, but by themselves they are likely to be incomplete and misleading. Ways of getting additional information, brought out in our discussion, include the following:

(a) Develop new quantitative measures.

(b) Ask "how are you doing?"

(c) Go and see.

(d) Use annual executive appraisals.

(e) Use staff as eyes and ears.

One member of the group reported that his company is working on *new quantitative measures* of such things as customer attitudes, employee morale, productivity, and executive development. The company feels that gathering and processing of data on these "intangibles" may be done more quickly and completely by the use of electronic computers. It is hoped that information now widely dispersed and difficult to analyze can be made available for management planning and control. Several other members said they believed much more could be done in developing quantitative measures of key factors now handled on the basis of impressions. There was general agreement, however, that these new measures were still in the experimental or embryonic stage.

The *"how are you doing?"* approach stresses a full discussion with the manager of a department. This discussion covers results achieved, major problems, long-range plans, etc. Reliance is placed on the manager himself to assemble the information needed to show how he is matching up to the established criteria. In other words, the top executive does not have a lot of control information passing over his desk so that he "knows at all times what is going on." Instead, the operating manager is responsible for deciding what records and reports he needs to run his department and to demonstrate his accomplishments.

"Ask him the things that will help him—or scare him, or stimulate him—to do his job right. . . . You have to ask questions that will cause him not to be complacent, but to consider his whole activities broadly. By less checking and more asking you show confidence in the operating manager. He'll like it a lot better and he'll work a lot harder."

One proposal was: "Ask the man himself to give you a picture of how well his division is doing. When he gets through laying out the criteria by which he measures his business and reporting on these, you will have a good idea of the ability of the man. We do too much relying on our own standards and making our measurements, and make too little use of self-imposed standards."

We need more study of this approach. It was noted, for example, that there is often an inconsistency between "decentralized, profit-and-loss-responsibility" and insistence on keeping elaborate and expensive accounting records. Even if the manager is "free" to decide what measures are most significant for his department, is he not likely to provide the kind of information which impresses his boss? If so, then is the essence of the approach how and when the reports are presented to the boss? The right climate and especially the relationship between the two men involved is vital to the success of the "how are you doing?" approach.

Several in our group did not accept the idea that top management could be as passive as stockholders, relying upon the department managers to tell their own story. Instead, they believe top executives should *"go and see."* More precisely, they recommend that the responsible executive should visit plants, stores, branches, etc., and ask questions of a wide number of people.

One member spends a week each year visiting customers, suppliers, and others who deal with his company, just visiting and asking questions. He feels that the information so obtained is vital to his appraisal of operations. Another insists that "the answer which is unpopular with gentlemen like ourselves is to get out of our chairs, and go out and see it rather than depend on paper or people coming to see us. . . . There is no better way than this face-to-face, travel-the-airlines method."

Mere visits are not enough. The top executive must be skilled in asking questions which get behind the polite and pat answers; he must also be skilled in really listening and interpreting the answers. To cite a case in point: "I recall one manager who was pleased with holding his share of the soap market. When I asked how he ranked in the entire cleaner industry, including detergents, he began to see his job in a different light. In fact, if that question had not been squarely faced until two or three years later the company would have been forced into a back seat in its industry." The art of asking discerning questions goes to the heart of appraisal of intangibles.

A related mechanism for getting information is the use of *regular executive appraisals.* Some companies have formalized these reviews and maintain reports on the work of each executive clear down to foremen. While these appraisals often emphasize executive inventory and executive development, they may give information on operating results. One member explained that his company asks each executive to make a semiannual written report on how well operations in his department were performed. These reports serve as a basis for personnel review and future planning. In a sense, they are a formalized way of asking "how are you doing?" discussed above.

This asking questions and listening takes time, and as noted in the preceding chapter, there is the inevitable problem of what part of his total energies an executive should devote to visits and personal contacts.

Still another way of getting information, and one which saves time of the top executive, is the use of *staff* assistants to gather and interpret data. This is common practice for accounting and statistical data. While there often are differences in opinion regarding the interpretation of such figures, their compilation is sufficiently conventional to permit delegation to staff.

Most of the members of the Round Table, however, were reluctant to rely on staff to appraise intangibles. This caution was due largely to two factors. (1) Control staff runs counter to decentralization. The staff naturally tends to bring more and more problems into headquarters. This creates an almost irresistible temptation for the chief executives—personally or via the influence of staff men— to mix into matters which have been delegated to the operating managers. (2) The personal contact and interaction between the chief and his key subordinates, already stressed in the paragraphs above, is sharply curtailed. In fact, when the criteria are not clear-cut, staff men may decide what performance is desirable as well as test the results. A blurring of standards and of responsibility is apt to result.

In most of these appraisal methods will be seen the active participation of the men being judged as well as executives making the final evaluation. When the managers themselves understand the criteria being used and take part in sizing up results, they are naturally more likely to hit the target. This again emphasizes the need (a) for clarifying what kind of performance is really wanted and (b) for avoiding measurements which give undue weight to certain results while glossing over others.

5

Size and Morale

IT IS SOMETIMES SAID that large size stifles initiative, leads to bureaucratic attitudes, and discourages young men with ambition. On the other hand, many men who possess outstanding ability are eager to work for large firms.

Clearly, any exploration of the management of big enterprises must consider how size affects attitudes and morale. In the Round Table discussions, we gave attention especially to the influence of growth on morale of key people—the junior executives, specialists, and "comers." Communications and the use of staff, having an intimate bearing on morale, were also considered.

Here, as in other areas, the Round Table sought insights based on varied experience, points of agreement and of difference, and leads for further study.

MAJOR FACTORS AFFECTING MORALE

The first observation was that size by itself is not a major determinant of morale. Examples were cited of both high and low morale in small firms, and similar differences were noted in large enterprises. In fact, one or two members advanced the proposition that size had a negligible effect on morale.

For instance, morale is often poor in a small company dominated by a president who insists on being a solo player. One member who had participated in the purchase of such a company commented, "I have never seen a more browbeaten, inadequate group of employees." Also, it was noted that a small proprietor-owned firm may have less balanced executives in key spots; here stock ownership and family connection often have more influence in selecting executives than ability matched against company need.

Even those of the group who were most enthusiastic about decentralization and small operating divisions cautioned against assuming that small size always leads to high morale.

One of the companies represented in the Round Table has many operating units. This company has experienced no clear correlation of size with morale among *key personnel*—if anything, there is better morale in the larger units, perhaps because of success and growth. However, as the operating units get larger than four or five hundred employees, it becomes more difficult to maintain good morale among the operating employees.

A variety of factors quite aside from size were reported as having a strong influence on morale, and especially morale of key personnel. Important among these are:

(a) *Management philosophy*—the treatment and attitude of executives in higher positions toward those beneath them. This does not mean a soft attitude. One member reported a study showing that executives who insist on high performance often have the greatest respect. But such insistence must be accompanied by fairness, objectivity, interest in building strong subordinates, making opportunities for promotion, giving credit where due, no niggardliness in bonuses if the company is able to pay them.

(b) *Success of the unit* and the entire company. A feeling of achievement, of being on a winning team, is contagious. The inevitable tugs and strains seem worth the effort when success is clear. On the other hand, it is hard to be enthusiastic about a rear-guard action when contraction is taking its toll.

(c) *Clean-cut organization* with clearly defined duties. A mutual understanding of who does what reduces confusion, empire building, and frustrations. It enables men to concentrate on given tasks with confidence that related actions are also being cared for.

(d) *Clear objectives and measurable results.* Self-assurance and sense of accomplishment are important factors in good morale. These are more likely to prevail when the goals—the missions—are sharp and progress toward them easily known.

(e) *A supervisor who delegates,* and then supports his subordinates. Most key men respond to the confidence implied by the assignment of a job to be done. This pride is enhanced when they feel sure their boss will back them up if the going gets rough.

(f) *Growth,* with its accompanying opportunities for advancement. "There's nothing like growth," said one executive. "Our divisions which are expanding most have lots of spirit, eagerness to tackle new problems, and, of course, plenty of room for men with ability. If frictions arise or mistakes are made they don't remain as festering sores but are soon swept into the background."

Several members of the Round Table granted that the foregoing factors have a more direct effect on morale than does size. Nevertheless, they contended that size was not insignificant primarily because of its indirect effects. "It may be possible to have all these favorable factors in a large enterprise if you work at it hard enough, but size in turn is a factor which makes it more difficult to achieve some of these things."

Again, "I agree that morale does relate primarily to the local situation; however, the local situation depends upon how big an organization it belongs to, how decisions are made in that organization, how objectives are set, how plans are communicated. . . ."

LARGE SIZE AS AN AID TO MORALE

Three ways in which large size may contribute to high morale of key personnel were noted:

(a) Identification with a large enterprise, well known because of its success, often is a significant factor in good morale. Employment with such a nationally known firm gives status with friends and neighbors.

(b) Large firms are able to hire good managers and staff advisers who keep abreast of the latest managerial techniques. Also, there may be greater objectivity in administration, including insistence on good personnel practice.

(c) Young and competent junior executives like to work for a large, growing enterprise because possibilities for vertical or horizontal promotion are more frequent.

These benefits of size may apply to either centralized or

decentralized companies. It is important to note, however, that mere size gives no assurance that the advantages will be present. A large, stable organization might offer none of these attractions to key men (e.g., some railroads and some government bodies hemmed in by obsolete civil service rules).

SMALL SIZE AS A MORALE BUILDER

Small size, on the other hand, may contribute to good morale. The reasoning here applies to decentralized units of a large enterprise almost as well as it does to a small company.

1. Several members of the Round Table felt that the "right management philosophy," noted above as a key factor in morale of any company, was easier to achieve in a small unit than in a large one. Complexity, more layers of supervision, greater reliance on technical staff, all tend to create an impersonal and hurried atmosphere in a big enterprise.

2. Smaller units tend to be simpler. This means that it is easier for all key people to see the results of their efforts. "The problem of identifying the subdivided labor of professional people in a large firm with the end result may well be at the root of communication, attitude, and morale difficulties."

3. Small, simple units are more likely to be staffed with executives equal to their tasks simply because the requirements of the jobs are not so exacting and there is a larger supply of men to draw upon. And, people are more comfortable and competent in doing things they "can get their arms around."

4. In smaller units where fact-to-face contacts are fre-

quent and informal, it is easier for an able leader to diffuse his personality throughout the organization. (Unfortunately, the impact of an inept executive is likewise strong.)

5. At least two companies have found that the key executives of decentralized divisions get highly interested in the success of their particular small unit. Their identification with their "own" operation is more intense and wholehearted than is the reaction of executives in large complex operations. Also, if the loyalty is primarily to the headquarters office, then men located one thousand miles away begin to feel isolated.

In summary, some members thought large size merely made the task of getting high morale different than in small firms; others contended it became more difficult. There clearly are *potential* benefits for both small and large firms if they are smart enough to capture them.

Perhaps the most striking feature of the preceding analysis is that the two lists of benefits are not mutually exclusive. It is possible for a large, decentralized company to have its cake and eat it too—provided other aspects of management are right! If the top executives insist on sound management practice within operating divisions and establish a tradition of company-wide promotions, then morale of key men throughout the enterprise may respond to company prestige, good supervision, and unusual opportunity. At the same time, the operating divisions provide face-to-face relationships, close contact with results, jobs that are doable, and a sense of an important role in "my" division.

Approached in this way, large size can be made an asset rather than a liability in building morale.

SIZE AND COMMUNICATION

Good communication, like good morale, bears no simple and direct relation to size. A vital factor in healthy communications is right relations between each man and his boss. This relationship is an intimate and personal one which either promotes a full and reasonably accurate exchange of ideas, or sets up barriers based on withholding of information and lack of appreciation of the other's point of view. The development of relationships favorable to communication is not a question of size—nor of systems and reports.

One member said: "The worst communication problems I have encountered have been in small companies. This happens especially in owner-managed companies in which there is a tradition of 'playing it close to the chest.' On neither side is there a willingness to communicate nor an appreciation of how to go about it."

But, assuming that these personal obstacles can be corrected, there is then evidence that increasing size does tend to upset good communications. In this connection, stress was laid on (a) complexity arising from variety of work and from (b) distance, as well as on (c) size measured in number of employees.

Most of our group agreed that greater size and complexity of operations made communications more difficult. Large firms can afford more specialists dealing with ever narrower problems, but this also means more people to contact before action proceeds. Such growth tends to multiply the problem of satisfactory contacts between individuals in geometric proportion. And, as already noted, poor communication leads to poor morale. In large and complex units, people get unhappy because they don't know what the score is, and because they don't know enough about each other's work to cooperate easily.

To some extent these difficulties can be overcome by modifying the communication processes. Formalized reports and memorandums must take the place of personal contacts to a large degree as a company grows in size and complexity. New communication skills can and must be developed, for without them growth would be impossible. But these formalized communications never completely do the job. Ideas must continue to pass through the minds of an ever increasing number of individuals.

The inevitable increase in layers of supervision with growth in size was noted. While it was admitted that many firms might well add to the span of supervision of their executives (thereby forcing more delegation), sooner or later the layers will have to be increased. This naturally makes communication up and down the line more complicated.

Experience of several members indicated that communication "up" is harder to achieve than communication "down." One explanation of this was that the boss does not hesitate to prod about in the work of his subordinates whereas subordinates are naturally more reserved in poking their noses into the boss's business. Another suggestion was that a subordinate has less basis for understanding the problems of the boss and knowing what to communicate than is true in the downward flow. By no means least is the inevitable desire of a subordinate to pass on only the things which will make him appear favorably in the eyes of the men who determine his salary and promotions.

The effective flow upward is likewise limited by the capacity of higher executives to absorb a mass of information.

The chief means of dealing with these communication difficulties which was discussed at our meetings is simply to reduce the information that needs to go up and down. In other words, avoid the problem to a considerable degree by keeping top executives aloof from details of operations. One member strongly urged that such "executive isolation" was, in fact, quite desirable because it permitted the top man to do the job which only he could perform. While there was general agreement that most bosses probably keep too much information flowing over their desks, we did not have time to explore just how isolated it is desirable for executives to become. As one president observed, "How far from the chain of events can a man be, and still not become an utter supernumerary?"

We need to know much more about the kinds of problems executives at various strata should deal with, and the ways they can obtain adequate information to make wise decisions on these problems. As pointed out in Chapter 3, guides on what an executive should *not* decide— and consequently the information he does not need—can simplify communications more than streamlined reports or assistants to predigest the welter of incoming facts.

FITTING STAFF INTO THE TEAM

Still another source of low morale is improper use of staff. Like communications, staff work is directly concerned with planning and with control, and consequently is also discussed in other chapters of this report. Here we are focusing on why staff sometimes interferes with good team play.

Members reported that a large part of the difficulty surrounding staff work comes from conflicting ideas and misunderstandings of the term itself. These differences are especially serious when new positions are set up or when executives are shifted from one job to another.

Part of the confusion arises because "staff" may be used to describe any of the following *types of work:*

1. Specialized reporting and advice to top management
2. General, personal assistance to an executive
3. Specialized advice to other executives on the same or lower level (e.g., not one's boss)
4. Performing "operating" work, such as actual purchasing or keeping accounting records

We quickly agreed to set aside from our discussion "operating" activities ("4" above), even though such work might be done in a central unit as a service for other departments. The desirability of such auxiliary service units is a separate issue, and not at the heart of problems concerning "staff." *

Even with auxiliary service divisions excluded, we still have the first three types of staff work noted above. All

---

* In passing, the conventional use of "line" as distinguished from supply, or auxiliary, departments was challenged. All such units do necessary work; none is concerned with planning the performance in other departments. Several other members felt that a distinction between major and auxiliary operating departments was useful, and that the somewhat illogical reference to major departments as "line" does not cause much confusion in practice. The difficulty arises when everything outside the major operating departments is called staff.

this remaining staff work is primarily concerned with planning or controlling the performance of people in *other* departments. That is, the staff man becomes effective not by managing his own subordinates but, rather, by influencing his boss or someone else's subordinates.

This concept of staff naturally raises questions of how the influence of a staff man is exercised. Several different types of *staff relationships* were brought out in the discussion:

(a) The staff man may take a passive attitude, giving advice only when his boss or some other executive asks for it. He is then like an outside lawyer consulted from time to time.

(b) He may feel responsible for a certain phase of operations; watch results and devise improved methods; and take the initative in promoting what he considers to be desirable changes. Broadly speaking, his normal method of promoting a change may be either (1) to advise his boss who presumably has line responsibility for the operation in question; or (2) to advise the people doing or directly supervising the operation, and then appeal up the line when important recommendations are not adopted.

(c) The man may be given "functional authority" with respect to certain phases of operations. Then the operating people are not free to act on their own judgment in these areas; instead they get orders from the man with functional authority, and they are expected to respect these orders as though they came from the line supervisor. In this connection, reference was made to military practice of permitting a staff man to issue orders "in the name of" the commanding officer.

When both the kind of work and the intended relationships of a staff man are clear, the results may be quite harmonious. Certainly there was no doubt by members of the Round Table that staff could be very effective. Most men testified, however, that in practice the use of staff was likely to be troublesome. The larger and more complicated the enterprise, the more apt were these frictions to arise.

Important among the reported difficulties with the use of staff were the following:

1. All too often the scope of work and the intended relationships of a staff man are not defined. As one member observed, "This gives rise to appropriation of power and authority as well as withdrawal from proper acceptance of responsibilities." Ambitious staff men, out to make a name for themselves, "carry the ball every chance they get." Unless checked by top executives, the initiative and even the accountability may slip away from operating men to their "staff advisers."

2. Frequently a staff man does two or more kinds of staff work and has different responsibilities for each. "You have to guess from his tone of voice whether he is checking up for the president, giving friendly advice, or proposing to take over the job on a service basis." These multiple assignments are a potential source of irritation; they are confusing and may lead to bad feelings.

3. One member feels that the reluctance of top execu-

tives to grant functional authority in specified areas, and make this authority clear to all affected, is a source of difficulty. "When the situation calls for it, there is no reason to shy away from functional authority. It is better to say that Mr. Jones has functional authority with respect to X, than beat around the bush."

4. A business enterprise is made up, not of inanimate parts like a machine, but of people. Consequently, a stable situation with relationships developed over a period of time may work well, whereas trouble arises when new people with different expectations are added to the scene. The promotion of an operating executive to a top staff job is especially dangerous, unless there is strong reason to believe he has the personal qualities needed and also the ability to change his habitual ways of getting things done.

5. A staff man may, in fact, exercise much more influence than intended because "everyone knows the chief will back him up and so he can act directly." Or, having frequent contact with the chief, he can influence promotions; he praises or plays down an executive according to the acceptance of his "advice." This influence may be subtle and even unconscious. As one member expressed it, "The problem is that the president considers this staff his advisers, and because they are advisers to both the president and operating heads, the operating head finds it difficult to conceive of their only giving *advice* to him."

6. Overlapping responsibilities may be given to staff men. The particular example cited was the introduction of a "control staff"—as developed in the Army Services of Supply—in addition to a Controller already charged

with evaluating and interpreting accounting reports. Possible reasons for such duplication suggested were (a) inadequacy of conventional accounting data for managerial needs (discussed in Chapter 4), or (b) preoccupation of the Controller with accounting records, tax returns, and other non-staff duties.

7. Staff sets up a tendency to centralize decision making—as noted in Chapter 2. "The experts at headquarters figure out the one best way, and typically try to get a directive issued setting this up as a standing operating procedure. At some stages of growth this may be desirable, but it gets large firms snarled up in rigid systems." "A sure way to break morale is to have a lot of rule books which in effect tell the operating man that he can't do anything new."

A key element in all of the foregoing difficulties is an inadequate understanding of the role "staff" is expected to perform. Written job descriptions may be a partial solution, but they cannot do the whole job. Particularly in connection with morale, attitudes toward people and jobs and ways of working together are involved. These highly personal reactions are not established by fiat but must be nurtured carefully.

Difficulties with staff occur in all sizes of companies. And, in all kinds of companies the remedy to this incipient source of poor morale starts with clear thinking about organization and careful selection of staff men. The difficulties are especially hard to overcome in large-scale enterprises because of the many people involved. The chief executive may not be in intimate enough contact with his various subordinates to sense annoyances and frictions, and he has only limited time to coach men and smooth out misunderstandings. In this respect, increasing size complicates the problem.

Repeatedly in this chapter, as in the Round Table discussions themselves, we have noted that there is no simple and direct relation between size and morale. Nevertheless, it is abundantly clear that company growth—especially to a large-scale enterprise—does change the management task of maintaining high morale. As a company expands, fresh and continuing thought should be given to how the "small-town" climate of an operating division can best be blended with the prestige and opportunity of a large firm, how communication channels should be modified to fit the changing situation, and how staff can be fitted into the team without upsetting initiative and enthusiasm.

6

Problems of Transition

RELUCTANCE to change, so widely recognized among rank-and-file workers, is also an important factor in adjusting the management of enlarged operations. Transition from one form of management to another creates problems of its own, and it is to these that this chapter is devoted. The discussion will be summarized under the following headings:

1. Recognizing the need for change
2. Is there an easy way out?
3. Top management adjustments
4. Adapting other executives to a new management philosophy
5. Revolution vs. evolution

RECOGNIZING THE NEED FOR CHANGE

One of the most critical stages in the growth of a company is when basic changes in management practice become essential. The first of these transitions occurs in a small shop at the time the skilled craftsman ceases being a doer and becomes a manager. A second basic shift occurs when the owner-manager can no longer personally keep track of the details of day-by-day affairs. He, or his successor, must learn to delegate and rely upon key men to direct each major activity. Budgets, reports, and other management aids are brought into play.

Still another critical transition comes when the single manager, even with the aid of staff assistants, can no longer give personal direction to the numerous operating problems of the expanding enterprise. The volume and diversity of issues calling for top-side attention become too great. Delays occur, snap judgments on inadequate understanding are made, reports go unread, what has been good management machinery now becomes cumbersome. Decentralization or some other new management philosophy is called for.

As one looks back on the history of a company, the need for such a change may be clear. But this is "Monday morning quarterbacking." Can the need be recognized when it first presents itself; or better yet, can it be anticipated?

The necessity for this final transition may arise from growth in sales of the same kind of products. As one member said, "An expansion of sales from $100,000,000 to $600,000,000, such as we had, brings with it so many problems that the chief executive cannot possibly keep track of operations as he had been able to do when operations were smaller." Another member noted that a decision to integrate, either forward or backward, often adds so much complexity that a change in type of management is needed. Also mentioned was growth to a point where additional plants are economically desirable. By no means least important, mergers often create the need for a type

of top management which none of the components pos-
sessed as separate enterprises.

All men present recognized that there is no single,
simple criterion of when a company has reached the point
that decentralized administration should replace one-man
management. Complexity of activities, geographic dispersion, rate of growth, ability of key executives, as well
as size, must be considered.

Perhaps the most striking point made regarding the
need for a change is that rarely do companies foresee this
need in time to prepare for it. Instead, the common situation is for firms to outgrow their old managerial practice
and find a change necessary for survival. In one company
the top executive decided to decentralize only when he
called a meeting of all men concerned with an operating
problem that he was impatient to solve—and found a room
filled with twenty-five people!

Loss of market position to competitors, financial loss on
certain parts of the company business, sheer exhaustion of
the top men, or a heart attack are usually necessary to
dramatize the need for a change in the management
set-up. The transition is likely to be painful and expensive,
so part of the hesitation to act may be a cautious "waiting
to see if it is really necessary." However, as one senior
executive observed, "We have never been smart enough to
project this kind of thing very far. . . . Pressure already
here made us do things we might have foreseen had we
been omniscient. I haven't yet found anyone who was
omniscient."

Several of the members of the Round Table believed
that although their companies might have been slow in

sensing the need for a change, they were now planning well ahead. And, a more widespread recognition of management transition as a potential problem may help other companies to foresee their needs.

IS THERE AN EASY WAY OUT?

Several cases were cited during the discussion of decentralized companies adding a new line without causing serious growing pains. A diversified manufacturing firm, for instance, sets up a team of men to develop a new product in all of its aspects—engineering, production, sales, finance—and when the product is ready to be marketed this team becomes the management group of a new division. Other companies deliberately develop an ample supply of "comers" so that executives may be moved easily into newly created divisions. Two instances of buying small concerns which became additional operating divisions were also mentioned.

In each of the above cases, however, the company had already "decentralized" and the new unit fitted easily into the existing management pattern. They are examples of growth, to be sure, but they did not create the need for transition described in the preceding section.

Another way of "taking growth in our stride" is to keep operations simple, sloughing off service and supply activities wherever possible. One of the "big three" automobile manufacturers followed this approach before the war. As it grew bigger, it became more simple. It had a deliberate policy of farming out everything except engine making and assembly. More recently this policy has been abandoned, and the company is faced with the problem of assimilating large and diverse operations. Nevertheless, for a period of years bigness was counteracted by the company's becoming less complex.

This approach has been applied by oil companies and in other industries. But it can be carried only so far. Simplification may be economically sound only to a limited extent, and the remaining operations are likely to be too large for one-man management.

Another possibility was mentioned in passing, namely, keep the company small enough for one man to run. This may well be the most practical solution where dominant individuals or other considerations make decentralization impractical. However, it simply evades the fundamental issue of how to deal with growth.

Consequently, members of the Round Table felt that basically there is no easy way to avoid a major transition. Once the operations of a company exceed the capacity of the top man to manage directly, a change in management approach is needed. In the opinion of our group, this change should be to some form of "decentralization," as explained in Chapter 2.

TOP MANAGEMENT ADJUSTMENTS

Once the need of a company for a basic change in management is recognized, the most critical part of the transition is the adjustment in behavior of the top executive.

This is no simple adjustment. Typically the top executive will have grown up in a centralized type of operation; the success and growth which now makes decentralization desirable is to a considerable degree the reflection of his ability personally to direct operations. Then the shift comes, and the top man is to "think and plan but not operate." The same types of problems continue to come up, but the chief executive is not supposed to hit the ball when it crosses the plate. Another batter has been assigned that job.

The necessary change in behavior of the top executive is as drastic as the shift in the quality of leader needed by a union when it passes from the organizing stage to one of mature bargaining.

The pooled observations of our group were that all too often the top man fails to make this adjustment. "In many companies we find that the chief executives understand intellectually the need to decentralize, and they have set up the organization mechanics to do it, but they have not in fact decentralized." They go through the motions of properly organizing but their behavior backslides every other afternoon.

Not infrequently the top executive tries to decentralize because other firms have done it, but he lacks conviction. Decentralization involves a spirit—confidence in other people, patience, a zest for teaching, willingness to share the limelight, and self-restraint. Unless the chief executive has this spirit along with a deep-seated confidence that decentralization will work, the company will flounder during the transition. As one member expressed it, "The top man has to have the gospel pretty deep or the change is going to run into trouble."

This need for conviction and spirit on the part of the chief executive may create a tough problem of transition. Subordinates can help sell the idea to him, but the necessary change in attitude and behavior must originate largely within the man himself. Fortunately the adjustment does not have to take place overnight. One of our elder statesmen observed, "If you decide to decentralize you have to let the men try it for three or four years. Then if the chief executive hasn't made the adjustment, you can't make him over. He either has it in him, or he hasn't." If he cannot adjust, either the trial decentralization has to be postponed or a new man put in the top executive position.

ADAPTING OTHER EXECUTIVES TO NEW MANAGEMENT
PHILOSOPHY

Just as the top man must learn not to make day-to-day decisions, so must his operating subordinates learn to shoulder the responsibility for such decisions.

While some subordinates welcome the opportunity to make their own decisions, others will resist it. Especially if they have been working for a "one-man operator," the natural tendency is to turn to the boss for major decisions. Again, more than intellectual acceptance of decentralization is needed. Habits and attitudes must be changed, and this calls for continual tutoring and experience.

One member told how, upon replacing a centralized operator, he resorted to making himself unavailable to subordinates who wanted him to make decisions just as his predecessor had done. He was always "tied up" when they called him on the phone. Even when he did talk with subordinates he forced them to make proposals which he promptly accepted. "It was not long until the problems were piling up on them and they had to make decisions." As a consequence, the subordinates learned they had to take the initiative and decide for themselves. Some mistakes were made but decentralization became a reality.

Another suggestion for encouraging operating subordinates to act like real managers is to give them offices and other physical trappings which look important. Two of the companies represented at the Round Table have recently reassigned office space and spent considerable money to show clearly that "here indeed is a big shot. There is no need to go further for a decision." This atmosphere of authority has an effect upon both the executive and those who come in contact with him.

Not all executives carried over from the old regime to the new will be able to accommodate themselves to the new philosophy. Transfers, early retirements, and discharges were all mentioned as ways of dealing with such individuals. In other words, part of the price of moving into a decentralized set-up is that some former executives may be misfits in the revised managerial pattern. The number and the appropriate treatment of such casualties will depend in part upon how fast the transition is to be made.

REVOLUTION VS. EVOLUTION

Speed of change. Reference was made during our explorations to companies which moved slowly and also those which decentralized rapidly. In fact, some firms have developed a decentralized management, not by conscious design, but through successive minor adjustments. Such evolution is, of course, a less painful and disrupting form of growth.

Two reasons stood out in our discussion why most companies cannot arrive at decentralized management via the evolutionary route. (a) Most small companies prosper and grow as a result of strong central management, and decentralization is a sharply different way of managing. Consequently, the likelihood of evolving toward decentralization is slight. (b) The need for change, as noted above, is rarely recognized until the pressures are strong and urgent. In general, then, there is not time for a gradual shift.

This means that the transition usually starts with a deliberate decision that positive action is necessary. Fundamental changes in habits and attitudes of all key executives are called for and this will not occur without top-side pushing and occasional use of the "shock treatment." In one large corporation which has recently taken decentralization seriously, for instance, the president not only announced the change to his associates; he has published the plan, made his remaining top staff preach the gospel, cut the size of the top staff units drastically, and otherwise made the shift very clear.

However, the fundamental changes cannot be brought about overnight by any such pronouncements. Every member of the Round Table who had been through a major transition testified that at least two or three years are necessary for a real adjustment in ways of thinking, attitudes, and personal relationships to take place.

Frequency of change. Related to the question of how *fast* a change should be attempted is how *often* major shifts should be initiated. One view on this latter issue was that a large enterprise cannot stand the shock of a new management philosophy more than once a generation (30 years). Adjustments to a broad philosophy of management is a long process. It requires (1) recognition of the prob-

lem, (2) selection of the philosopher—for example, Sloan
in General Motors, (3) selection of the people, (4) conditioning them all the way down through various levels of
the organization, and (5) the impact on every aspect of
the business—product-line, facilities, etc. "You can't make
a complete change of this sort in less than thirty years, and
there is no reason why you should."

There was not full agreement that the transition period
needed to be so long, but it was the consensus of the group
that basic changes should be soundly enough conceived
so that major revisions are unnecessary for periods of at
least a generation in length.

The two preceding paragraphs deal with a "basic change
in management philosophy." There is still the question of
whether the shift should be attempted as one major step,
or in a series of moves. Companies represented in our
group have followed different paths in this respect. Experience shows that frequent changes may lead to a sense
of instability, when men feel insecure and wait for the
next reshuffle rather than work hard in their present positions. Clearly, if frequent changes in organization or other
mechanics are really frantic attempts to cover up human
deficiencies, they merely add confusion to weakness.

On the other hand, under good leadership there may be
a ready acceptance that modifications at least in organization are a normal response to new operating conditions.
Also, successive moves that are clearly parts of a recognized plan cause less disturbance than unpredictable shifts.
For example, one member explained that his company is
facilitating the transition from a functionalized set-up to
decentralized product divisions by the use of product com-

mittees. Men concerned with a particular product in research, production, sales, and finance are placed on a
committee responsible for that product (and there is sufficient delegation to them to permit action). Work on this
committee prepares the men to be executives of the new
product division when it is established; in fact, the men
soon see the advantages of decentralized operation and
urge that the shift be made.

Specificness of change. The final aspect of evolution vs.
revolution considered was the extent to which the new
ways of management should be written out. Some members felt that it is impractical to spell out the relationships,
attitudes, planning procedures, and other facets of decentralized management in a detailed manner for a specific
company. These things, they contended, grow up like the
common law, and shift with replacements in personalities
and pressures of the times.

Other members suggested that written expressions of a
new management set-up should not be considered as stat-
utes, for this would introduce inflexibility and provide
spotty coverage. Nevertheless, there is grave need for
mutual understandings in a newly decentralized company,
and the writing down of some guides—be they only a
rough approximation of canon law—may contribute to
these understandings.

The value of the written statement, one man said, is
90 percent in the thinking and exchange of views which
are required to prepare the statements. This assumes, of
course, that the executives affected take an active part in
framing the statements. "In a company which changes, no

one knows quite where to go, and an executive cannot depend on past habits. To think through the rules shortens the period of gestation."

These observations indicate clearly that a growing company should consider not only *what* changes in management practice are desirable but also *how* to make the transition.

7

Decentralization in Government and Highly Integrated Establishments

THROUGHOUT this report has run the recurring theme of decentralization. Again and again the Round Table discussions stressed decentralization as a way of managing large and growing enterprises.

Not all firms, however, are well suited for decentralization. It may be difficult to divide their activities into distinct operating units; or, their activities may have to be so closely sychronized that independence of action cannot be granted to each division. Also, we were frequently reminded that the standard pattern does not always fit government work. This naturally leads to the question:

> To what extent can the benefits of decentralization be secured in large integrated companies and in government?

The exploration of this question also provides a further opportunity to test previous conclusions.

THE DECENTRALIZATION CONCEPT

A brief review of prime features of decentralization, which have been set forth earlier in this report, will be useful in answering this question.

An essential step is the separation of work into operating divisions. Each of these divisions is very much like a small business in itself. It is self-contained or self-sufficient in that it has within its orbit the performance, or at least control over, all of the major activities necessary to make a profit. Moreover, it is granted a high degree of independence in the course it chooses to follow, being confined only by broad company policies and review of major decisions. And, as a natural consequence of such scope and independence of action, it is held accountable for profitable and otherwise satisfactory results.

Successful operation of these decentralized divisions requires certain attitudes and work habits of executives in both headquarters and the divisions. The division executives must take the initiative on any matter they believe affects the success of their particular division. They must consider direct and indirect results of their actions, and not rely on someone else to provide the balanced, discerning check on their proposals. In short, they should possess a sense of stewardship for the economic resources put at their disposal. And they must be willing to take action and stand by the consequences.

Operating divisions staffed with such competent executives free top management from day-to-day operating problems. In a decentralized set-up, the senior executives can concentrate on broad, long-range issues and give only general direction to the heads of operating divisions. This freedom, however, is an obligation as well as a privilege. Top executives must develop a "hands off" attitude toward the decentralized divisions. This calls for confidence in the capabilities of other people, a belief in teaching rather than telling, patience while others are learning—perhaps through their own mistakes—and a willingness to let others stand out in the public eye.

Many problems arise, to be sure, in the application of this general concept of decentralization even in multi-product companies. Several of these problems have already been discussed in preceding chapters, and others are noted in the Appendix. Nevertheless, Round Table members gave ample testimony that decentralization can be of immense benefit to a large and diversified firm.

Why is this successful management concept not applied to government where large-scale operations also prevail?

DECENTRALIZATION IN GOVERNMENTAL OPERATIONS

A common misconception. Decentralization is far more common in government activities than is ordinarily realized. One speaker's impression was that "by and large, government operations are decentralized to a very substantial extent." Another stated: "Government as a whole, national, state, and local, is more decentralized than we assume." He gave the example of the public school systems of which there are some 7,000 in the country—"each pretty much the master of its own fate." Likewise, port and highway authorities are "almost autonomous corporations which are left alone so long as bonds can be sold and the facility kept open." Subway systems are also of a "proprietary nature, closely analogous to business."

There seems to be no reason why decentralization cannot exist widely in such units. The factors responsible for lack of decentralization in other government bodies are not nearly so applicable to these "proprietary units."

In the national government the Armed Services are the leading examples of decentralization, both in peace and in war. Theater commanders and ship captains have full authority and responsibility within the scope of their mission. It was noted, however, that these officers have been subject to a large amount of indoctrination before "being turned loose." This makes it safe to decentralize, because of assurance of a standard pattern of behavior.

Factors limiting the extent of decentralization in national government. While considerable decentralization does exist in the Federal government, largely as a result of work by the Bureau of the Budget and other groups in the executive branch, this approach to management is not generally followed for several reasons:

1. The frequent intervention of Congress is a strong restraint. In order to carry out its legislative function, Congress inquires into the actions of all branches of the government at all levels. This constantly raises the possibility of exposure and criticism of every act of both minor and major officials, and it means that a large amount of information about the reasons behind particular acts needs to be ready so that questions about the act can be answered. Congress can demand explanations and get into the details of "what someone way down the line did." Decentralization is inhibited by such checking.

Besides its need to investigate for legislative purposes, Congress has political reasons for influencing the extent of decentralization. In order quickly to answer detailed questions brought by the voters, Congressmen prefer to have all the records at the Washington headquarters of an agency. As a result, the heads of departments and agencies are greatly concerned with knowing exactly what is going on and intervening in anything that is of interest to Congress. This is vital because the acts of minor officials can suddenly become of major importance to the job of the chief. It was stated: "The Secretary of State must almost take personal responsibility for the specific acts of a minister in any one of fifty different capitals. The individual act may be blown up into an issue which is the life and death of a governmental executive." As long as Congress can call on government administrators to explain every act of their own subordinates, there will be a great obsession with knowing what is occurring at all levels.

2. Outside groups put pressure on government departments in addition to the influence of Congress. "Clients," such as the American Legion and the Farm Bureau, have easy access to executive departments and often intervene in special decisions. As another example, it was said that shippers and carriers can intervene in the decision making of the Interstate Commerce Commission. The head of an agency, who must answer to the clientele as well as to Congress, has a strong inducement to centralize decision making. "The president or the governor or the mayor has to protect his flanks and his hands and feet much more than does the chief executive of a corporation simply because access to decision making is open to many more interveners. . . . Isolated acts would not be held to such strict accountability in the life of a corporate executive." It was held that business has no real parallels to this

intervention in specific decisions by the clientele or Congress. Shareholders are disenfranchised from interference in operations. One member said: "The stockholder has certain rights which are highly restricted. He is only protected against the directors in those instances in which the directors abuse their trust and he does not vote on a nose-count basis. He has access to records on a limited basis. He cannot remove the director or manager for an error in judgment. He has no right to interfere in the operation of the business. He can only ask questions of the board. Thus business develops under a different thesis than government."

3. The absence of (a) an impersonal mechanism such as the market place and (b) a widely understood criterion of success such as the profit-and-loss account also inhibits decentralization in government. Lacking the profit-and-loss control, Congress gets interested in detailed decisions. Evaluation of the over-all results of an administrative unit is not easily achieved and, therefore, control often is attempted by supervision of individual decisions and not by review of the results of those decisions.

This lack of a common goal, one member felt, leads to a difference in the objective and in the "charter" given to a governmental administrator. "The charter given to the Secretary of Defense is not to defend the country, but to defend it with so many divisions, so many air groups, so many people, hired under certain pay scales. The charter is one to perform a specific objective, but hemmed in with all kinds of administrative restrictions, limitations, and caveats. . . . In all those limitations and restrictions the electorate is reflecting itself, for good reasons and bad. The

objectives of a Congressman are not confined to the objective of national defense."

4. The length in office of policy makers and chief executives deters decentralization. Mayors and governors stand
for reelection at much more frequent intervals than do
corporate executives. It was said that the necessity of getting reelected frequently "puts a very great premium on
short-range and expedient policy as compared with the
kind of planning and thinking that business would do."
Although the actual management does not change as often
as is indicated by the election period, there is little basic
long-term direction except self-protection.

5. Problems of bureaucracy are likely to work against
decentralization. An ingrown civil service may neither
understand nor want responsibility pushed down the line.
These attitudes of the bureaucracy arise from several
conditions which one speaker stated "made public administration different and more difficult" than business
administration. His points were: (a) limited salaries for
higher positions, (b) lack of economic as distinguished
from professional training for public servants, (c) slowness of promotion, (d) slowness of changes in operation,
and (e) emphasis on safety of position. Such conditions
tend to emphasize preservation of the "status quo" and
limit the willingness to take responsibility. (As noted in
Chapter 6, difficulty in getting people to accept responsibility is often a limiting factor in the extent of decentralization.)

6. When local offices are filled through patronage, the
top executives are reluctant to decentralize. For instance,
"postmasterships are the dollar bills of patronage for representatives," and the resulting inability of responsible of-

ficials to choose their key executives explains, in part, why 10,000 post offices report directly to Washington.

Conclusions concerning decentralization in government. These restraints on the use of decentralization do not mean that there is no carry-over to government administration of the practices developed in industry. The particular concept of decentralization of responsibility for operations and for profit making may not be applicable, "but this is not to say that there is no alternative concept or no way to do more." Conferees agreed that the conclusion could not be drawn that government cannot be more decentralized than it is. The feeling was, however, that government would probably always lag behind industry in the application of decentralization.

Lessons for business. Discussion of decentralization in government brought out some important implications for business administrators. Legislative and political requirements of Congress, activities of "clientele agencies," and the requirements for control all made for extensive intervention in the particular decisions of government administrators either by outsiders or by the chiefs of the executive branch. The influence of this on the behavior of the individuals should be clearly noted. (1) "The government administrator spends his time building alibis for his defense." (2) "The possibilities of public criticism make necessary a paper record for each insignificant act." (3) "Fear is created all the way through so that no one does anything that he thinks he might be criticized for."

The executive who is subject to all this outside pressure and criticism for his possible lapses of judgment does not take risks but instead uses his energies making sure that his defenses are sound. This process will naturally tend to destroy initiative and inhibit the willingness to take responsibility or the desire to try something out of the ordinary.

One member explained what similar investigative and censuring behavior on the part of a business executive will do to his organization. "People at the top who demand explanations and want to get into the details of what someone way down the line did defeat decentralization in business. The president of a steel company who wants to know why #9 open-hearth furnace in plant number so-and-so poured fifteen hours tap to tap instead of nine requires everyone down the line to get that kind of explanation and there is a great preoccupation with knowing what has happened and with being sure that the things that the boss is concerned with don't happen." The time and talents of the executives are used in finding excuses and answers.

A second conclusion—growing out of those turnpike, bridge, military, and other operations where a substantial amount of decentralization does exist—is that "profit-and-loss responsibility" is not an essential aspect of decentralization. The goal of the operating unit may be some other mission.

However, if the mission of a government agency is not clear-cut and widely accepted or if the results are not measurable, there is an understandable tendency for top officials (or Congress) to intervene in the operations and to question minor actions.

DECENTRALIZATION IN HIGHLY INTEGRATED COMPANIES

The Round Table also explored how the benefits of decentralized management might be secured in large, integrated operations which cannot be divided into small independent units. Previous discussions had centered around decentralization in companies which could be broken up into product or area groups and in which profit responsibility could be readily established for each unit.

Not all business enterprises can readily establish separate operating units with as much freedom of action as has been granted in the examples cited. The size and complexity of the end product, such as aircraft or electric generating equipment, may prevent separation of the plant into independent units. In some cases a single marketing organization may be much more economical and effective than several distinct sales forces. In industries such as steel, oil, and aluminum, technology dictates a minimum operation of sizable proportions (though not necessarily as large as the biggest firms in those industries). Automobile production apparently is more economical in very large volumes so that heavy costs of tooling and special part fabrication may be spread over many units.

Do these technical factors mean that decentralization cannot be used? That is, when for some reason activities must be closely integrated and freedom restricted, is centralized management the only course to follow?

Testimony of members of the Round Table was that the principles, or at least the general philosophy, of decentralization can be applied to these integrated operations. The concepts can be used if special attention is given to:

(1) approximating independent, competitive conditions in so far as possible;

(2) carefully defining the points where coordinated action is vital, and allowing freedom in other areas;

(3) adjusting measures of successful performance to fit the results which are wanted.

Simulate profit-and-loss conditions. A division may be run "as if it were an independent business." One firm with a large plant, for example, has put its in-plant railroad on a profit-and-loss basis. The railroad manager negotiates rates for his services with the various divisions and makes extra charges for special services. The negotiations are much like an I.C.C. hearing, with all pertinent facts and comparable outside rates presented as evidence. As a result of this set-up, "the divisions that are being served know where they can make complaints and have their problems solved. The railroad manager, at the same time, has improved service and become very cost conscious. Instead of acting like a glorified switchman, he is now a railroad executive. He looks at all aspects of his business—procurement, management, equipment, service, and everything else."

A similar arrangement has been created for electric power. The power division must charge rates in line with those of outside power companies. Moreover it tries to earn a return on investment in power facilities comparable to well-managed outside companies.

In neither of these cases is the service division allowed to refuse service or to seek outside income. Nor are its "customer" divisions free to buy from anyone else. Nevertheless, the spirit and point of view of an independent enterprise has been created—with salutary results.

Other examples of semi-independence were brought out in the Round Table discussions. Where volume warrants, two plants making the same product may be given wide

latitude on many things, except product design and speci-
fication. In aircraft production, parts making is often put
under different management than assembly. Models or
projects can be separately managed. In each instance, a
clear attempt is made to approximate independent, competitive conditions.

The fact that two or more independent units operate
within the confines of one plant need not bar such decentralization. "We had several departments in the same building or on the same floor, and merely put imaginary fences
around them."

Define points of coordination. The preceding examples
show that it is entirely possible to split off portions of an
integrated company. Giving such portions an independent
status, however, does raise major questions of coordination
and of measurement of performance—especially when
captive suppliers or restricted markets are stipulated.

Output of the separate parts must be unified in some
way, and the interests of the entire corporation must receive recognition. One speaker stated: "There is the question of coordination at the low and distant levels of parts
of a big company operating nationally. This coordination
is needed voluntarily and directly between the units in
order to avoid laddering up and down. This is one of the
restrictions on an integrated organization as opposed to
a decentralized product organization in which your coordination is needed less often and is easier to effect."

Three complementary ways of achieving action in ac-
cord with company-wide interests came out of our discussions.

(a) The first is to define and write down the corporate

policies. Once written they become the "rules of the game," and it is necessary for the operating executives to abide by them in order to secure the advantages of integration. One member explained: "We restrict our supply houses to our own products in certain lines, plumbing, bathtubs, and things of that kind. Still it is decentralized and set up under separate divisions. This is the kind of policies that we were talking about. Our people complain that they lose business by not being able to break the package and sell roughing material or something else when a competitor's unit is specified. They complain, but that is just one of the rules."

In return for this sacrifice of freedom, the operating manager "takes a ride on the company name which helps in dealing with customers and attracting employees. The enterprising manager, we hope, thinks it is a fair swap and loses none of his initiative and enthusiasm."

(b) Relationships must be clarified. Operating units of an integrated company obviously cannot be given the autonomy of a self-contained end-product division. There is need for a clear understanding of what actions should be coordinated with whom.

As one member explained: "Our blower division lost a big order last week because they neglected to work with the motor division on a combined proposal to the customer. A competitor, who offered a package, beat them out." Another need for united action was reported: "I spent a lot of time last week appeasing a customer who had been cut off by one of our subsidiaries because he was so unimportant to them, but he is very important to another of our divisions."

The remedy in neither of these cases is to centralize control. Rather, working relationships should be defined. Each executive should know: What kinds of actions may I go ahead with, and what kinds should be checked with someone else? Whom should I consult? Is this problem so important that joint agreement must be reached, or is it a voluntary matter?

Some members felt that definition of these interrelationships would go a long way toward solving the problem of coordination. Such definitions are, however, more difficult to establish than are the definitions of ordinary duties. "On job descriptions, the relationship responsibilities are customarily slipped over or poorly defined. . . . As we have enterprises in which the relationships are more complicated, we must spend more time thinking out what the relationship responsibilities are as contrasted to the functional responsibilities."

(c) Often the chief points of coordination can be confined to specifications, volume and delivery dates. This is true for a division supplying parts, and in some cases for a manufacturing division transferring goods to a sales division. Other aspects of administration, such as personnel policy, need not be uniform or integrated throughout the company.

The fact that an operating division is part of an integrated enterprise does not greatly change scheduling problems. As one member said, the answer to the output question is to learn to schedule against the requirements of the ultimate user. "In an independent firm you make your schedule against the end-product movement. All you do in these larger enterprises is to push the end of the process out further. You look at the movement of the goods not on the assembly line but from your captive distributor to the retailer, or, if you own the retailer, from the retailer to the final consumer. The same principles apply as you learned long ago in the factory." This type of scheduling between operating units within a company can be done just as it is with independent suppliers or customers.

Integrated action, then, of several operating units can normally be achieved by a clear statement of policies, careful definition of relationships, and intelligent scheduling based on projected sales to the final customer. More significant, it was the consensus of the Round Table that operating divisions could "live within such restrictions" and still have a feeling of being an independent enterprise.

This sense of full responsibility will be secured, however, only if the restrictions are kept to a minimum. Also, the attitudes and actions of top executives must be like those already stipulated for successful decentralization.

Adjust measures of performance. A prime requisite of decentralization is holding the manager of an operating division responsible for results. His freedom of action, his self-sufficiency, must be matched with accountability. What can be said of the manager's responsibility in a division of an integrated company where sharp limitations have been placed on freedom of action?

The existence of captive suppliers and restricted markets is a significant qualification to decentralization in integrated companies. One unit is forced to buy from the other. Is either component really free? With such restrictions will the manager feel that he is responsible for the operation of his unit, and will his performance approximate that of the manager of a decentralized product unit in the generation of enthusiasm and initiative?

"A major difficulty we find for these kinds of components of integrated operations," one speaker said, "is the lack of an easy measure of accountability such as a clear and simple profit statement."

One approach is to approximate a profit-and-loss situation. As in the instances of the in-plant railroad and the company power plant already described, each division may be put in a position as close to independent competition as possible. Then the manager is held accountable for profitable return on investment.

Since it is often necessary to insist that buying be done from sources within the total enterprise in order to avoid idle resources, the question was raised as to the real negotiating power of the "buyer"—his ability to apply pressure as he would to an outside supplier. The buyer may have only the negotiating power of disclosure, but at least in some companies this has proved to be effective. "He can develop all the data available to him and lay it on the line. . . . The man running the power plant is confronted with the demand to know why he cannot sell it cheaper than someone else. The man to whom he reports has to answer that question. The answer may be, 'I guess we need a new manager.' The power plant manager knows this. That is an effective sanction."

A related device is used by some companies which have separate divisions produce most of the parts used in their final assembly. A small portion of each part is bought from an outside supplier. The price, quality, and service of these outside suppliers are used, along with an estimated profit, to appraise the effectiveness of the captive plant. This is done year after year because a captive source may fail to keep up with competition. Equipment, originally the best available, may become obsolete and an assured market may lull division management into complacency. The outside check keeps the management on its toes, and gives validity to the profits test.

But, the division within the integrated company may be asked to do things and render services not expected from an outside supplier. One member stated: "The greatest difficulty comes because no definition has been made of whether the objective of a decentralized component is to make a profit in its own area or to maximize sales and profits in the over-all company. It should be defined."

The sharper the objectives and the simpler their fulfillment is to measure, the more likely is decentralization to succeed. We have already noted in Chapter 4 that profits are an inadequate standard for semiautonomous divisions. It is not unlikely that as more comprehensive measures are developed for these units, we will be able to use some of the same tests for divisions of integrated companies. This will be possible, however, only if the results each division is expected to produce are clearly defined.

Absence of a simple profits test need not bar decentralization. One member said that this restriction was merely another example of the "owner's interest" which needed to be defined, but, once defined, could be accepted as another statement of policy. "Your question is, can you get the same enthusiasm in successive units of an integrated, vertical operation as you would if they were under separate ownerships? The common ownership tends to bring about a community of policies among the components. This is a valid point but not an unmanageable one. If you face up to it and define your rules, you can accomplish substantially the same thing you can with separate ownership."

Decentralization, an expanded view. The sharp conclusion which grows out of this discussion is that the essential aspects of decentralization are applicable to integrated firms. The concept of decentralization previously developed is easy to understand, but it may have been oversimplified. "In a sense we have been too narrow in our definition of a way of managing found to be effective. Apparently we can set up a unit of operation, even within integrated companies, with sufficient freedom to get much the same result as with a self-contained unit."

The experience in integrated companies, along with that in government, suggests that decentralization is possible when:

(1) *The goal or mission of the operating unit is clear.* This may be maximum (estimated) profits, dependable supply of good water, a winning baseball team, or speedy and safe delivery of goods. As soon as objectives become complex and fuzzy, there will be a natural tendency to centralize control and to take part in day-by-day operations.

(2) *The unit is essentially self-contained and independent* in the actions it takes to achieve its mission. There can be "rules of the game" in the form of policies, stipulated relationships, and derived output schedules. However, these must be limited in number and scope, and leave wide discretion to the local manager. These restrictions should

be more concerned with defining the goals than with methods of performance.

(3) *Results are appraised specifically in terms of the mission.* If desired results are immeasurable, or some aspects are measurable while others are not, decentralization may lead to inefficiency or a mild form of anarchy. On the other hand, when the chief executive can easily check results he feels safer in decentralizing.

These three conditions are permissive, but they are not the essence of decentralization. They leave out the attitudes and the spirit. The capacity and willingness of top executives to assign major tasks and then keep hands off, and the balancing eagerness of division managers to take the initiative and carry responsibility must also be present. "It is not necessary to think of decentralization always in terms of a fairly autonomous profit center with a minimum of relationships with other components. This is an idealized set-up. You move back from that to a fairly integrated set-up, and yet can retain all the benefits of your profit center system in this integrated set-up. It requires more skill, better understanding, understanding that there are more reserved powers. . . . I don't think there is any difference in principle."

Decentralization, then, is more nearly a philosophy of administration which may, with skill, be used in many forms of large-scale enterprises.

Appendix

Areas Needing Research—
Challenge and Opportunity

Our Round Table discussions were intended to be exploratory in nature. They gave much more attention to diagnosis than to prescription. The procedure at each meeting was designed to bring troublesome issues out in the open. It was only natural, then, that many more questions were raised than were answered.

The more important of these questions are summarized in this Appendix, because one of the principal aims of the Round Tables has been to identify areas of management needing careful research. The questions which arose in our informal give-and-take discussions give some excellent leads for further investigation. They reflect problems that experienced and successful administrators have found vexing.

The questions which follow do not represent a comprehensive and systematic analysis of the "management of expanding enterprises." Instead, they are problems which kept bobbing up in the course of our study. Some partial answers are given in the body of this report, but in the main the questions represent a challenge and opportunity for men who believe improvement in our knowledge of management is a highly worth-while endeavor.

TOP MANAGEMENT IN A LARGE ENTERPRISE

1. What should the chief executive of a large company do that men below him need not do? Should these distinctively top

management duties be modified as the firm increases in size?

2. How does the top executive who has delegated responsibility for operations let go of operating decisions and supervision? How does he turn that task over to his subordinates and make it stick?

3. What are effective working methods for a chief executive? What kinds of problems should he worry about? Which should he decide? Whom should he consult? How does he get action? What should he do about mistakes and lack of action? What kind of information should flow to him regularly? Whom should he keep posted? What restraints should he observe? In what ways can he best make his influence felt?

4. How does a chief executive know when he is paying enough attention to current operations, and when he is paying too much?

5. To what extent should "chief executive" duties be performed by a team of two or more men? How can such a team concept be developed? Can the full benefits of a top management team be obtained without weakening the spur of clearly identified, personal responsibility?

6. As a company grows, do the qualities needed in its chief executive change significantly? What can be done to help top executives adapt to shifting requirements of their jobs?

ADAPTING THE ORGANIZATION TO INCREASING SIZE

1. As a company grows, how can the need for coordination and also a high degree of delegation be reconciled? When is decentralization feasible?

2. How does the form of expansion affect the organization needed? Should growth at a single location be treated the same as the addition of more units (plants, stores, or offices) doing similar work in other locations? Does the addition of a new product line call for still a different adjustment?

3. What are the essential features of decentralization? How does it differ from delegation to a foreman or other supervisor?

Can it be applied to giant government undertakings? Is it applicable to parts of an integrated operation?

4. To what extent should decentralized units be self-sufficient? What are the factors and the conditions which justify continuation of central services (legal, purchasing, industrial relations, real estate, research, and the like) in a company with decentralized operating units? What are the most effective relationships between such central services and operating units?

5. Should activities be split as finely as the size of a firm will support, or are there limitations other than size which make ever narrower specialization undesirable?

6. How can flexibility be achieved in large-scale operations? This relates to sensitiveness to shifting needs, speed of change, and cost of the adjustment.

INFLUENCE OF COMPANY GROWTH ON PLANNING

1. Does an increase in size of a firm mean that more people must be consulted before a decision can be made? Is more attention necessary to the communication of data needed for decision making? How does company growth affect the level or strata at which any given kind of problem should be decided?

2. Should the form of the plans be changed as a company grows? Should procedures be spelled out in greater detail? Should traditions be written down as policies? Can general guides replace detailed review of budgets? Is a shift from stress on method to emphasis on broad objectives and annual goals desirable?

3. Does increasing company size make long-range planning more practical? More necessary?

4. Does the meaning attached to the term "policy" change as a firm expands? What kinds of problems should be covered by policies? How detailed and specific should they be?

5. How "autonomous" should decentralized divisions be in their planning? As the company grows should this freedom of decentralized units to make their own decisions be increased?

CONTROL WITHIN GROWING ENTERPRISES

1. How does remoteness, which is inevitable in large-scale enterprises, affect the nature and the detail of standards to be used in appraising performance? What type of standards should be applied to decentralized operating units? To service units? To functional units such as engineering or sales?

2. How can intangible factors be measured when direct, personal observation is no longer feasible?

3. What guides are most useful in anticipating trouble—in fire prevention?

4. What are the most effective methods in growing companies of finding out how well standards are being met? How obtain a balanced summary of results and build a forward taper into reporting systems? What can a top executive do to avoid bias in the information reaching him?

5. Should the strictness and closeness of control vary inversely with size? Under what circumstances should the maxim "Don't get into the act. If results are bad, fire the man" be applied?

6. To what extent can control be secured through indoctrination, careful selection of men for promotion, and other indirect ways of shaping the thoughts of subordinates?

EFFECTIVE USE OF STAFF

1. As an enterprise grows, how can staff men continue to be close enough to the top executive so that they really serve as an extension of his personality? If this close touch is lost should staff units be retained at a high level in the company, or should their functions be decentralized?

2. What top management duties are most suited to the use of staff assistance? Union negotiations? Capital budgeting? Long-range planning? Financial negotiations? Public ceremonies and speeches? What role should staff play in such matters?

3. Should staff be kept in a purely advisory position, or should top executives also use staff as an aid in control? If staff assists

in control, can a truly advisory relationship be maintained with operating men? How avoid staff being regarded as spies?

4. Does the use of staff undermine the initiative and sense of responsibility of operating executives?

5. When the same kind of staff units (e.g., accounting, personnel, sales promotion, legal) are set up in both the headquarters and the operating divisions of a large firm, what is the most effective relationship of the local staff man to (a) the manager of the operating division and (b) the top staff man at headquarters? Does "loyalty to profession" cause difficulties?

EXECUTIVE SELECTION AND DEVELOPMENT *

1. How does size of a company affect the kinds of executives needed at various organization levels? For example, are different social skills needed to work effectively in large enterprises? How does size affect the task of discovery and development of such executives?

2. How are executives qualified to run large-scale enterprises to be found? What is the best system for picking them? How test them? How determine that they are ready to make their own mistakes?

3. How can, say, a sales manager who is forty-five years old be reoriented to become a general manager? How can the viewpoint and attitudes of an expert in a specialized technology be shifted to that of a long-range thinker, planner, organizer, and teacher? What types of training prepare a rising executive for new and unforeseen jobs?

4. In what ways do the personal qualifications of a staff man differ from those of an operating executive? What is the best training ground for staff men? Should they be moved back and

---

* Executive personnel was not a major topic at the Round Table on Management of Expanding Enterprises since a similar series of meetings devoted entirely to this subject were being held concurrently (see Eli Ginzburg, *What Makes an Executive? Report of a Round Table on Executive Potential and Performance,* Columbia University Press, 1955). Nevertheless, some basic questions regarding executive personnel inevitably arose.

forth from operating jobs to staff jobs? Are there better ways to get "practical" staff men?

EFFECT OF COMPANY SIZE ON PERSONAL ATTITUDES

1. Does increasing company size provide employees additional opportunities for personal initiative? Is there a stage in growth when obstacles to individual initiative counterbalance the greater opportunities? How can the entrepreneurial spirit be cultivated?

2. How does large size affect the ability of a firm to provide the following motivations for its members: prestige, security, self-confidence, self-expression, desire to compete, power, creation, financial income?

3. Are employee attitudes toward their work and their employer affected by company size? Is the danger of bureaucracy serious in large enterprises? Is a penny worth saving? How can personal identification with company objectives be retained by people remote from the chief executive? Does complacency accompany the security offered by a large, successful company?

4. What arrangements, formal and informal, can be made to overcome communication difficulties as firms grow? How avoid isolation of departments, branches, top management?

5. How can growth be used best as a morale builder? What can be done to maintain morale when a company stops growing? Is it desirable to try to change attitudes toward change?

GROWING PAINS

1. What are the signs that company growth has reached a stage where a basic change in the type of management is needed? How can such a need be forecast far enough in advance to permit an orderly readjustment? Are there any serious dangers in long-range organization plans?

2. What are the best ways to make a transition in type of management? How do you get people to adjust to and embrace a new management set-up? For example, in a division which has

just been decentralized, how does the manager accustom himself to his new relationship with the chief executive?

3. Is reorganization necessarily bad for morale? Should reorganization be used to keep men on their toes, or to emphasize a change in policy which calls for readjustment in personal attitudes?

4. What should be the timing of a management transition? How rapidly is it possible to make changes? Does the need for stability limit the frequency of change which is desirable? Are some occasions better suited to change than others?

5. Can management structures be designed which may be rapidly expanded or contracted? Should aircraft and other "defense" companies, for instance, make special provisions for sharp changes in volume? Can effective informal organization and social relations be established by people who regard change as normal and perhaps fun?